Household Hints

by Anne Cope

Illustrated by Craig Torlucci

A Nitty Gritty Book*
Published by
Nitty Gritty Productions
P.O. Box 5457
Concord, California 94524

*Nitty Gritty Books — Trademark
Owned by Nitty Gritty Productions
Concord, California

Printed in USA
Mariposa Press
Concord, California 94524

ISBN 0-911954-54-6
Library of Congress Card Catalogue Number:
79-92446

nitty gritty books

Chicken Cookbook	Soups & Stews	To My Daughter With Love
Skillet Cookery	Crepes & Omelets	Natural Foods
Convection Oven	Microwave Cooking	Chinese Vegetarian
Household Hints	Vegetable Cookbook	The Jewish Cookbook
Seafood Cookbook	Kid's Arts and Crafts	Working Couples
Quick Breads	Bread Baking	Mexican
Pasta & Rice	The Crockery Pot Cookbook	Sunday Breakfast
Calorie Watchers Cookbook	Classic Greek Cooking	Fisherman's Wharf Cookbook
Pies & Cakes	Low Carbohydrate Cookbook	Barbecue Cookbook
Yogurt	Kid's Cookbook	Ice Cream Cookbook
The Ground Beef Cookbook	Italian	Blender Cookbook
Cocktails & Hors d'Oeuvres	Cheese Guide & Cookbook	The Wok, a Chinese Cookbook
Casseroles & Salads	Miller's German	Japanese Country
Pressure Cooking	Quiche & Souffle	Fondue Cookbook
Food Processor Cookbook		

designed with giving in mind

Table of Contents

The Nitty Gritty of Coping

There are the experts in this world . . . and then there are the rest of us. We have to know a little about so many things to cope with our lives—from cleaning house to all the paperwork of modern living. These are hints to help you along the rocky road to better living through small gestures . . . tips to help you manage more efficiently and to keep you and your hard-earned dollar together longer.

The battle cry of the 80s might be "use it up, make it last, wear it out." When resources are scarce and prices up, our only salvation is to take care of what we have and take charge of what we can.

Someone once said that maintenance is the hallmark of a civilization. Our throw-away society needs to relearn that lesson, not only in caring for our things, but in caring for ourselves, too. It is the combination of small gestures that can help us all live better.

Housekeeping

Most of us want to live in organized and reasonably clean surroundings. The problem is: How do we achieve this with a minimum of time and effort? Supermarkets are filled with products that claim they will do the jobs for us easily and quickly, no rubbing, no buffing.

The truth is, 99 percent of these products will do a good job, but at exorbitant costs. When you realize, for example, that you can make your own window cleaner for about 1/4 cent per ounce (yes, you read it right), you may be downright mad at what you've been paying. The story is the same for almost every product sold.

Whether you like your house immaculately clean, or simply give it that well known "lick and a promise," these tips will help you accomplish it cheaper and faster.

Cleaning

Brass

1 Unlacquered brass that is badly tarnished can be cleaned in a solution of 1/2 pint vinegar plus, 4 tablespoons of salt and one quart of water. Mix it up in a plastic container. Soak small pieces overnight. Then rinse in clear water, wipe dry and polish with a soft cloth. Large pieces can be rubbed with a cloth which has been soaked in 1/2 cup warm vinegar and sprinkled liberally with salt. Rinse in water and polish dry with a clean, soft cloth.

Pewter, Brass and Copper

2 Pewter objects can be cleaned and brightened with a paste made from equal parts of salt, vinegar and flour. Coat all surfaces and allow to remain for an hour. Then, scrub with an old toothbrush, rinse in water and dry. Polish with a soft cloth. This works well on brass and copper too.

Silver

3 Here are two improvisations that will do nicely when you're out of silver polish:
- Use toothpaste as polish. Rub, rinse and polish just as you would with silver polish.
- Place silver in a ceramic or glass dish and cover it with sour milk. Let it stand overnight. Rinse each piece in cold water. Polish with a soft cloth.

Chandelier Cleaning

4 Here is an easy way to clean a crystal chandelier. Put a few towels on the floor under the chandelier and spread several thicknesses of newspaper over the towels. Cover each light bulb with a small plastic bag and tie with a twister or a rubber band to prevent any water from getting into the sockets. Spray enough window cleaner on the crystal so that the dirt runs off the chandelier onto the floor. The crystal can drip dry or you can dry it with a soft cloth for more shine.

Porcelain and Glass

5 All those little washable treasures that seldom get washed, such as porcelain and glass objets d'art, can be placed on a tray or in the sink and sprayed with window cleaner. After spraying them thoroughly, move them to a towel to air dry.

Two Household Cleaners

6 Here are two all-purpose household cleaners that you can make yourself. Both can be used to clean floors, walls, tubs, tile, woodwork and more.

- Stir 1/2 cup ammonia and 1/3 cup washing soda (sal soda) into a gallon of warm water. If you are washing floors and walls, you'll need it all. If you store it for smaller jobs, be sure to label the container.

- An even easier mixture is 2 tablespoons of trisodium phosphate (TSP is available in paint and hardware stores) in 2 quarts of warm water.

6

Cleaning Wallpaper

7   Make this dough-like substance to clean smudges from wallpaper. Dissolve 1-1/2 pounds of salt and one ounce of aluminum sulphate (alum) in one quart of water which has been heated to 180 degrees F. Remove mixture from heat. Add one ounce of kerosene and slowly sift in 2-1/2 pounds of flour, stirring to prevent lumps. Turn dough out onto lightly floured board. Knead until dough becomes smooth and less sticky. That way it can more easily be rubbed onto the wallpaper. Place unused portion in a plastic bag and close it tightly with a twist tie. Store mixture in an empty coffee can.

Cleaning Oil Spots on Garage Floor

8   Kitty litter is great for absorbing those oil spots on the garage floor. Just sprinkle it on, wait a few hours and sweep. Sand or dry soil from your garden can be substituted for kitty litter.

Mops

9   Keep your cleaning mops from becoming stiff after you use them by adding a capful of fabric softener to a pail of water and rinsing them thoroughly in it. A mop that is soft and fresh-smelling is almost loveable.

Furniture

Dusting

10   Here are two ways to make your own treated dustcloths that will pick up dust and leave a nice shine on your furniture:

- Add two teaspoons of turpentine to a jar of hot sudsy water. Put in a few soft cloths and screw on the lid tightly. Let them soak overnight. Then hang them up to dry and they are ready to use. When they become dirty, wash them as you would any other rag. Then recondition them again in the above formula.
- Dip soft cloths into a solution made from one pint of hot water and 1/2 cup kerosene or lemon oil. Dry cloths and store in a tightly covered metal container, such as a coffee can.

Dents

11   A shallow dent in a solid wooden surface can often be raised by laying a damp rag over the dent and gently moving a warm iron across the top of the rag. Be careful not to scorch the surface by letting the iron get too hot or by leaving it down too long.

Burns

12   Cigarette and other burns can usually be rubbed out of wood with a piece of fine sandpaper. If the burn is shallow, use artist's oil paints or shoe polish to color the area to match the rest of the surface. Re-polish the entire piece of furniture when the "touched-up" area is dry.

13   Some burns can be lightened with a dry steelwool pad. Use caution, however. It must be done with some judgment. Rub lightly and check the results frequently as you work. It may be necessary to "touch-up" the area as described in the above hint.

Candle Wax

14   If candle wax has dripped onto your table, first carefully scrape off as much as possible with a dull knife. Then, holding a clean blotter, or several thicknesses of paper towels over the spots, lightly rub a warm iron back and forth over the towels. The heat will soften the wax and the towels will absorb it.

Scratches

15   Felt patches glued to the bottom of ashtrays, ornaments, tables and chairs will keep them from scratching wooden surfaces.

16   Sometimes an oily nut meat, such as walnut or pecan, cut in half and rubbed on a light scratch will cover it. If the wood is dark, iodine may conceal the scratch. Use this sparingly, however.

17   Minor scratches can often be covered with a compatible color of shoe polish.

Watermarks

18   Watermarks or white rings on furniture may be removed with a very fine abrasive such as silver polish or toothpaste. Another good method is to use a mixture of salt and salad oil. First dip your finger in the oil; then in the salt. Rub the stain gently, then polish to restore the luster.

Alcohol Rings

19   Liquids containing alcohol are apt to dissolve varnish and make permanent rings. Wipe up spills immediately and rub the spot with your fingers. Treat old stains with a paste made of rottenstone (available in hardware stores) and a little lemon oil. Rub the paste in well. Wipe the area clean with a soft cloth.

Heat Marks

20   White patches, usually heat marks, can be rubbed with a mixture of equal parts of turpentine and linseed oil. Rinse with vinegar and repeat the process until the mark is gone. Rub dry with a soft cloth.

Piano

21 Here's where **NOT** to place your piano: near radiators, air vents, sources of heat, next to or in front of a window, or against an outside wall. That leaves the middle of the room!

22 A mixture made from 2 parts lemon juice and 1 part salt will brighten your piano keys. Simply sprinkle enough of this solution onto a soft cloth to get it damp. Gently wipe each key on the piano with the treated cloth. Dampen another clean cloth slightly with water. Wipe each key again, removing cleaning solution. Thoroughly dry keys with still another clean cloth.

The Bathroom

Color Coding

23 In a busy family bathroom, a color coding system is a good idea. A different colored plastic cup and matching toothbrush for each member of the family will reduce confusion. You might even extend the code to include towels.

Toilet Paper

24 Here is the final authoritative word on the correct way to install a roll of toilet paper: The paper should roll off the front of the roll. You'll notice that the patterned paper is printed so that the pattern is right side out when it comes off the front of the roll. I ask you—would those people get it wrong? Case closed.

Toilet

25 If you want to get all the water out of the toilet for a thorough cleaning job, quickly dump a pail of water into the bowl. It will flush out, leaving the bowl empty.

26 Borax will keep your toilet bowl clean and odor-free without adding an unpleasant, antiseptic odor of its own.

Removing Shower Mold

27 Spray your shower weekly with chlorine bleach. It will keep black mold from creeping between the tiles. Let it stand a few hours and rinse it off before stepping in. Yes, the smell is strong, but it beats those sessions with a toothbrush and tile cleaner.

Shower Curtains

28 This is the simplest way to clean a plastic shower curtain. Put it in your washer alone. Use a high water level. Add 1/2 cup detergent and 1/2 cup water conditioner to remove the soap residue. Wash about five minutes. Put a cup of vinegar in the last rinse water and it will dry soft and pliable. Remove and hang to dry.

Get Rid of Bathroom Odors

29   When you want your bathroom to smell heavenly in a hurry, fill the washbasin with hot water and add a few drops of your favorite cologne. Let it stand until you need the basin.

De-fog Mirror

30   A quick way to de-fog the bathroom mirror after showers is to turn you hand-held hair dryer on it. The hot air will blow it clear in a few minutes.

Step Savers

Upstairs-Downstairs

31   Hang a tote bag or a basket at the head of the stairs in your house and another at the bottom. It's a good system to stow things for the next trip up or down the stairs. Far safer, too, than piling things on the steps.

Folding Sheets

32 If you fold your freshly laundered sheets lengthwise first, you'll know exactly where the center is when you make the bed. This handy trick will save you from making three trips around the bed in an effort to get the sheet on evenly.

Divide Housecleaning Into Sections

33 Divide your housework into imaginary sections. Most people find it easiest to do one room at a time. However you organize yourself, finish one section before moving on to the next. If you work aimlessly, you'll miss an area or waste time by going over the same section twice.

Small Pillowcases

34 Did you ever try to force a pillow that is too large, into a pillowcase? Try turning the case inside out. Put your hands in and grab the corners of the case along with the corners of the pillow at the same time. Flip it over and you've got it started.

A Case for Long-life Bulbs

35 Long-life bulbs cost more and produce less light per watt than regular bulbs, but in hard-to-reach places their convenience makes them worthwhile.

14

Gaping Draperies
36 If your draperies gap in the middle when you close them, sew a small magnet into both of the center seams. Then simply press them together for a tight closing.

Floors

Damp Mopping Wood Floors
37 To damp mop a wood floor use clear, warm water. Dampen the mop and wring out as much water as possible. Mop a small area at a time and wipe thoroughly dry before moving on to the next area.

Wax Buildup
38 Commercial products to remove wax buildup are expensive while this one does the trick for mere pennies. Wet a small area of the floor with a strong solution of about 1 part ammonia and 20 parts warm water. Let it stand for five or ten minutes, then scrub with a plastic scouring pad. Wipe up and proceed to the next area. When you've done the entire floor, rinse it with clear warm water.

Wax Withdrawal

39 Think about this: You and your floor can survive nicely **without** waxing! Consider these points:

- It is the quality of the floor and the amount of traffic it gets, not waxing, that determines its longevity.
- You can learn to love non-shiny surfaces.
- No wax build-up.

16

Windows

Spray Cleaner

40   Here's the formula for making your own window cleaner for pennies instead of buying an expensive blue mixture. Add 1 tablespoon of white vinegar and 3 tablespoons of ammonia to an empty 8 ounce spray bottle and fill with water. You can even add a few drops of blue coloring if you like. You'll have an economical way to make windows sparkle and kitchen appliances shine.

Washing

41   Get organized at window washing time. Use vertical strokes to clean the window. Have a helper dry the window with horizontal strokes. That way you'll avoid streaks. The job goes twice as fast too.

Dry With Newspapers

42   Instead of drying the windows you've washed with expensive paper towels, try drying them with newspapers. There is a chemical in the newsprint that makes windows shine.

Window Shades

43 A window shade that won't roll up to the top can be given new energy by pulling it down, almost but not quite to its full length. Then remove it from its brackets and reroll it by hand, not more than two revolutions. Now just replace it in the brackets. Repeat this procedure until the shade has the right amount of zing.

44 A window shade with too much "snap" to it can be tamed by rolling it up to the top and removing it from its brackets. Unroll not more than two revolutions. Then, replace it and roll it up again. Repeat this procedure until the shade rolls up the way you want it to.

Caring For Your Carpets

Professional Cleaning

45 Most rugs and carpets need a professional cleaning once a year. It's important not to let a carpet get too dirty.

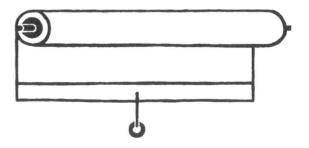

Treating Spills

46 The first step in dealing with carpet spills is to move fast and blot up (don't rub) as much of the spill as possible. Then treat the following stains with a solution made from 1 teaspoon of dishwashing detergent and 1 cup of water. Dry the dampened area quickly with more blotting or use your hair dryer.

alcohol	wine
tea or coffee	fruit and juices
soft drinks	ice cream
blood	medicines
eggs	candy
foodstuffs	chocolate

47 The following spills respond best to the use of cleaning fluid:

cosmetics	grease or oil
ballpoint pen ink	shoe polish
fats	

Check the label on the cleaning fluid for detailed instructions.

Sticky Messes

48 To remove candle wax and chewing gum from a rug, wrap an ice cube in a cloth and hold it on the spot until the substance hardens and can be lifted off. Then go over the spot lightly with cleaning fluid.

Pet Stains

49 To treat pet stains on carpeting, blot up as much as possible, then sponge the spot with plain or carbonated water. Make a solution of 1 part white vinegar to 3 parts water. Dab this on the stain. Dry thoroughly. You may have to use the detergent-water solution, mentioned in the following hint, and follow it with another application of vinegar and water.

Burns

50 Don't despair, cigarette burns in your carpeting can be professionally rewoven or retufted if they are deep. If the burn is superficial, carefully snip off the charred ends with sharp scissors. Then dab the spot with a solution of 1 teaspoon dishwashing liquid and 1 cup of water; blot frequently. Let the spot dry. Then go over it again with a solution made from 1 part vinegar and 3 parts water. Blot and dry.

Stairs

51 If you are carpeting stairs, it's a good idea to buy an extra foot or more of carpet. Fold this extra length in under one or two risers at the top of the stairs. When wear appears on the stair treads, shift the carpet down.

Candles

Easy Lighting

52 Lighting candles in glass hurricane lanterns or other deep holders that are hard to reach with an ordinary match can be accomplished with pasta. Light a strand of spaghetti (it takes a few seconds), then light the wick.

Firm Fit

53 If your candles are too big or too small to fit into your candlesticks, try one of these tricks:

- Soak the bottom 2 inches of the candle in hot water for a few seconds.
- Hold the bottom of the candle over a burner which has been set at medium-high. Leave it there for just a few seconds.

Then, insert the candle into the candlestick and hold it there for a while, until it's firmly seated.

Dripless

54 Chill candles in the refrigerator for 24 hours before using them. They'll burn evenly and will not drip.

Soiled

55 Soiled or finger-marked candles can be cleaned with a soft cloth moistened with denatured alcohol.

Closets

Prevent Dampness in Closets

56 Keep a 60-watt bulb burning in a damp and musty closet, but not where it could come into contact with clothing and create a fire hazard. Heat from the bulb will be enough to raise the temperature and help dry out the moisture. For a long-term solution, check into insulation, a dehumidifier or spraying the walls with a mildewproof preparation.

Easy Glide Hangers

57 It only takes a few minutes to wax the poles in your closets. It's so easy you'll wonder why you didn't do it before. The hangers glide along smoothly, and if the pole is painted, the wax will preserve the finish.

Fireplaces

No Mess

58 Avoid the mess the next time you have a fire. Cover the bottom of the fireplace with a big sheet of aluminum foil. When the fire has burned out, carefully lift the foil, gently shaking the debris to the center. Fold up the mess and dispose of it.

Odors

Smoking

59 If you're trapped in a room with smokers and the odor is distressing, try one of these ideas:

- Place a small bowl of straight vinegar somewhere in the room where it's not likely to be seen or spilled.
- Burn a candle or two.
- Open a window.
- And for the more flamboyant, wring out a towel in equal parts vinegar and hot water and wave it above your head as you walk through the room.

Pleasant Aroma

60 Short of baking a cake, you can still have a pleasant, spicy aroma pervade the entire house: Simmer 3 teaspoons of ground cloves in 2 cups of water for 15 minutes.

Kitchen Smarts

Whether you're in and out of the kitchen as quickly as possible, or you enjoy lingering, you need kitchen smarts. You need to know how to get the most for your food dollars, how to keep the vitamins in the food you purchase and how to care for all the shiny equipment that surrounds you. Learn how to avoid becoming bedazzled by clever packaging and labels with extravagant claims. It's amazing how one shopper can check out at the market with so much real food, while another, for the same amount of money, has not bought the makings of one good and nutritious meal.

Success in a frugal kitchen often depends upon your ability to improvise and substitute. And, even if money is not a problem, doesn't wasting food seem just short of criminal to you?

The following hints will make it easier for you to operate on a budget, in addition to increasing your kitchen smarts.

The Good Egg

Freshness

61   To test an egg for freshness give it a shake; if it rattles it's stale. If placed in water, a fresh egg will sink to the bottom; a partially stale one will rise slightly at one end; a completely stale one will float.

Separating

62   Eggs separate easiest when cold, straight from the refrigerator. It's best to let the whites warm up at room temperature for about 45 minutes before beating them. You'll get more volume that way.

Room Temperature

63   Eggs should be at room temperature when you are adding them to a yeast mixture. If they are cold they'll slow down the action of the yeast.

Whites First

64   When a recipe calls for eggs to be separated and beaten, beat the whites first if you plan on using them within 15 minutes. Then, without washing the beaters, beat the egg yolks.

Copper Bowl

65 The miraculous action that occurs when egg whites are beaten in a copper bowl with a wire whisk will work only if whisk and bowl are immaculately clean. Wipe both with a cloth dipped in vinegar before using. True, using a whisk is not as easy as pressing a button on your mixer, but this method results in more volume, and makes you feel like you're really cooking!

Freeze Leftover Egg Whites

66 Don't worry about wasting leftover egg whites when a recipe calls for the yolks alone. Collect them in a freezer container, or an ice cube tray. One cup equals seven or eight egg whites; one cube equals one egg white. They freeze well for up to 6 months. Use them for anything except angel food cakes, which depend upon fresh, room temperature egg whites for their success.

27

Hard Boiled

67   To slice hard boiled eggs without crumbling the yolks, first dip the knife in water. Then gently press the knife around the entire circumference of the egg, cutting only the white. The egg should now easily separate into 3 pieces: 2 halves of white and 1 whole yolk. With the knife, chop the white as finely as you wish. Don't attempt chopping the yolk. Simply pick the yolk up, hold your hand over the dish in which the yolk is going and press the yolk firmly. It will crumble into pieces.

Cookies

Gift Idea

68   Here's a sweet gift for an elderly neighbor or single friend. Make batches of basic cookie dough (oatmeal, sugar or peanut butter) and divide them into margarine tubs or other containers with lids. Tape baking instructions to the top and store them in the freezer for a quick snack or a spur-of-the moment gift.

To Soften

69   To soften hard, dry cookies, put them, together with a piece of bread or apple, into a tightly closed container. Replace the bread or apple every few days. Or, if you lack either bread or apple, try a dampened paper napkin wrapped in punctured aluminum foil.

Mailing Cookies

70   The best way to protect cookies when you're mailing them is to wrap them individually in plastic wrap. If this seems too troublesome to you, simply enclose 5 or 6 cookies in a plastic bag and close them securely. Next, sprinkle a couple of inches of popcorn on the bottom of the box you intend to ship the cookies in. Place one or more plastic bags filled with cookies in the center of the box, on top of the popcorn. Sprinkle the popcorn around the sides, and on top of the cookies. Make sure to fill the corners of the box. Add enough popcorn to reach the top of the box, so that when it's closed, the cookies won't rattle around.

Fruit

Bananas

71   When bananas are too ripe for eating and you don't have time to bake banana bread or cake, here's what to do: puree them in your blender or food processor. Freeze the puree in 1 cup batches. It will turn a little dark, but the wonderful flavor is not impaired.

Strawberries
72 Wash strawberries **before** hulling them. They will retain more of their sweet juice that way.

Peaches and Nectarines
73 To peel peaches and nectarines, dip the fruit into rapidly boiling water for about 15 seconds. Remove them with a slotted spoon and dip them immediately into cold water to prevent any cooking. The skin will peel off easily.

Citrus Fruits
74 The white membrane of citrus fruits is more easily removed if the unpeeled fruit is soaked in hot water for a minute or two.

Vegetables

Steam Vegetables
75 Steaming is one of the best ways to cook vegetables. There is no leaching of nutrients and the vegtables tend to keep their flavor, color, and crunchiness.

Potatoes

76   Let's hear it for the potato! Dieters often pass it up as being too fattening, but it is actually the victim of guilt by association: those rich toppings. A small baked potato is only 90 calories. It's a great appetite appeaser, costs little, and provides key vitamins and minerals, especially if you eat the skin. On an ounce-for-ounce basis, potatoes have fewer calories than rice.

77   Grated potato makes a good thickener for stews that are too thin.

78   Here's a way to bake potatoes in less time. Cut them in half lengthwise and place them, cut-side down, on a lightly greased baking sheet. Bake for 35 minutes in a 425 degrees F oven. When you're using those large baking potatoes a half a potato per serving is usually ample.

Rice

79   One cup of raw rice becomes three when cooked.

80 You can cook rice for dinner as much as a day ahead. When you are ready to serve it, put the cold, cooked rice in a colander that fits down into a saucepan. Simmer the water in the bottom of the pan, but do not let the colander touch the water. Put a lid over the colander. The rice will heat and the grains will separate nicely when stirred with a fork.

81 Don't wash rice before or after cooking, because some of the vitamins will be washed away.

A Pinch of Sugar
82 Add a pinch of sugar to frozen vegetables while you are cooking them. It gives them a fresher taste. Contrary to what you might think, it doesn't make them sweet.

Carrot Curls
83 Here's how to make a carrot curl. Use a potato peeler and cut long thin strips of carrot. Roll the curls around your finger, fasten them with a toothpick and drop them into salted ice water. Refrigerate for one hour. Remove toothpick and voila—perfect curls.

Cabbage
84   When you are boiling cabbage, add a piece of rye bread to the water. It will eliminate the odor. The trick is remembering to have rye bread in the house whenever you cook cabbage.

Parsley
85   Parsley will stay fresher longer if you put it in a jar with a tight-fitting lid and keep it refrigerated.

Tomatoes
86   It is best not to ripen tomatoes on a sunny window sill because direct sunlight will quickly deteriorate them. Warmth, not light, ripens tomatoes. The warm top of your refrigerator will do the job nicely.

87   Fresh tomatoes keep longer when placed with the stem end down.

88   Tomatoes are easy to peel if you let them stand in boiling water for 2 minutes first.

Mushrooms

89 There are a number of poisonous mushrooms, all quite innocent looking. If you bypass the market and pick your own, you would do well to remember the old maxim—"there are bold mushroom hunters and old mushroom hunters, but no bold old mushroom hunters."

Pimientos

90 Leftover pimientos won't spoil if covered with cooking oil and refrigerated.

Ginger Root

91   Many stir-fried dishes call for fresh ginger root. Unfortunately, it is sold in larger pieces than a recipe ever calls for. Here's what to do with the leftovers: Peel the unused portion and place it in a jar. Cover it with dry sherry and refrigerate. The sherry doesn't change the flavor of the ginger root. It should last over 4 months.

Tea

92   Make iced tea this cold water way and you'll never have cloudy results. Combine 4 cups of cold tap water and 8 tea bags in a glass or ceramic container. Cover and refrigerate overnight. Remove tea bags, stir and serve on ice.

93   On a chilly afternoon, add a modest drop or three of rum (say 1/4 of a cup) to your pot of tea and pour an aromatic cup of cheer. A household hint to warm the heart.

Chicory

94 With coffee prices where they are you might want to try a coffee extender: chicory. It contains no caffeine and costs much less than coffee. The distinctive taste may not appeal to all, so start slowly. It's available from you local coffee and tea importer.

Popcorn

95 Keep your popcorn in the freezer or refrigerator. This retains freshness and helps eliminate those "old maids."

Cheese

96 Don't be confused by recipes that call for Farmer, Cottage, Pot, Baker, or Hoop cheese. They are almost identical to one another. It all depends on what part of the country or world you're from and whose grandmother wrote the recipe. These cheeses are low in fat but high in carbohydrates.

97 When shredding soft cheese, like Monterey Jack, they will stick less if you wipe the grater first with a dab of butter.

98 A bit of mold that may have developed on cheese in the refrigerator doesn't mean it's spoiled, for heaven's sake. Cut off the mold and eat away.

Gravy

99 A pinch of salt added to flour before it is mixed with liquid will help keep gravy from becoming lumpy.

100 If your family likes gravy often, here is a "gravy starter" you can prepare in big batches. Mix 1/4 cup of soft margarine and 1/4 cup of all purpose flour together well. Add one tablespoon of bottled brown sauce which is made for gravy (Kitchen Bouquet is one such sauce). Add this mixture, a little at a time, to hot liquids and cook, stirring constantly, until liquid thickens. Use about 2 tablespoons of this paste per cup of liquid to be thickened. Refrigerated, this starter will keep for over 2 months. It's nice to have it on hand for stews, soups and pot roasts.

Yeast Dough

101 To raise yeast dough when the room is cool, set the covered bowl of dough in an unheated oven. On a shelf underneath, place a large pan of hot water. Replenish the water once or twice as it cools. Or, you can place a wire rack across the top of the pan of hot water and set the covered bowl of dough on it.

Prevent Boilovers

102 To prevent gummy boilover of noodles, rice or spaghetti, add 2 teaspoons of cooking oil to the water before cooking and your problems are solved. Noodles will glisten and separate easily.

Measuring Sticky Liquids

103 To measure sticky liquids such as molasses, honey, corn syrup, or sweetened condensed milk, lightly grease the inside of the measuring cup or spoon. The liquid will pour out cleanly.

Sticky Cuts

104 When cutting marshmallows or dates, the job will go faster if you dip your scissors in water and cut while they are wet.

Baking

105 If you bake a cake in a pan made of glass, porcelain-coated metal or any dark-colored aluminum or steel, set your oven

38

25 degrees F lower than your cake recipe directs. These materials absorb heat more quickly than plain aluminum.

Sinking Fruit
106   Nuts and fruits won't sink in the batter if you dust them with flour before adding them.

Food

Storage
107   Don't let anyone tell you that you must cool foods to room temperature before refrigerating them. It's a risky practice and major cause of illness from food.

Spoilage can occur rapidly between the temperature of 40 degrees F and 140 degrees F. It's best to put the warm food directly into the refrigerator.

108   Spices, herbs, coffee and tea should all be stored in air-tight containers away from light. Those decorative counter top glass jars are attractive but not the place to keep products that deteriorate in light.

109   Contaminated food often looks, tastes and even smells no different from good food. Remember, when in doubt, throw it out!

Shelf Products to Refrigerate

110   Some products that most people store on the shelf, are better refrigerated after opening. Peanut butter, shelled nuts and syrups are protected against becoming moldy or rancid if they are refrigerated.

Freezing Whipped Cream

111   Did you know you can whip cream and freeze it in individual serving portions? Cover a cookie sheet with waxed paper. Put dollops of whipped cream on the sheet and set it in the freezer until they are hard. Then place the frozen dollops in a freezer bag and store in the freezer to be used as needed. It takes about 20 minutes at room temperature for a topping to soften.

Buttermilk Substitute

112   A handy substitute for buttermilk when the recipe calls for some and you're out: Put 1 tablespoon of vinegar or lemon juice in a measuring cup and add enough whole milk to bring the liquid up to the 1 cup line. Let mixture stand for five minutes to allow it to thicken a little.

Scorched

113   To save scorched food, plunge it into cold water before transferring it from the burned pan to a fresh one. The burned taste is greatly lessened.

Herbed Vinegars

114　Herbed vinegars are expensive, but it is easy to make them yourself. Bring one quart of vinegar to a boil. Remove the saucepan from the heat and add **either** 4 teaspoons of dried herbs **or** 2 cups of fresh herbs. Tarragon, rosemary and dill are all good. Pour the herbed vinegar mixture into a large glass or ceramic bowl or bottle. Store it at room temperature for a week, stirring at least once daily. Then simply strain the herbed vinegar and bottle it. Attractive bottles of this make perfect gifts.

Brown Sugar

115　If you find your brown sugar has become hard, here's what to do: Remove it from its container and put it in an oven-proof dish. Place it in a 300 degrees F oven for about 3 minutes, or until just softened.

Potpourri

Rolling Pin Substitute

116   Are you new to the fascinating and expensive business of equipping a kitchen? If you have decided to postpone the purchase of a rolling pin indefinitely, here's what to use instead: a wine bottle. Chances are you'll have one of those around your house somewhere. If not, maybe now you'll have a good excuse to buy a bottle.

Brown Baggin' It

117   A "brown bag" lunch that can't be refrigerated and won't be eaten until hours after it is packed, can be made safe with one of these methods:

- Freeze the meat sandwich the evening before.
- Double wrap the sandwich and pack it with a cold piece of fruit or cold can of juice.
- Put something very cold in the bag such as a plastic bag filled with ice cubes, or an empty margarine tub filled with water and frozen.

Save Plastc Bags in a Cannister

118   Almost everyone saves plastic bags from the market to re-use. But they don't need a whole drawer by themsleves. An empty shortening container or coffee can will hold a lot of bags and leave the drawer free for more important things.

Plastic Lids as Coasters

119 Those plastic lids from coffee or margarine containers are terrific as coasters under bottles or oil or syrup in your kitchen cabinets. No more sticky rings that make shelves look messy.

Hot Liquids Into Glass

120 When you're pouring hot liquids into glass, put a metal spoon in before pouring to absorb some of the heat.

Knives

121 If you want your knives to hold a good edge, never wash them in the dishwasher.

122 Knives should be stored separately so the cutting edges will not become dulled by knocking against each other.

Glasses with Nicks

123 A very small nick in the rim of a drinking glass can sometimes be smoothed out with an emery board.

Placemats

124   Vinyl or straw placemats that are too large to fit into a kitchen drawer without curling will stay smoothly together if they are clipped into a trouser hanger. You can hang a whole set together in one hanger.

Grease Fire

125   To put out a grease fire in a frying pan, slap a cover on the pan. If you try throwing flour on the fire you may be burned by spatters.

Improvise a Cooler

126   Here is instant improvisation when you don't have a cooler for a picnic. Fill a plastic bag with ice cubes and put it in a coffee can. No ice cubes? Carry frozen juice packed next to the sandwiches and perishables. Insulate the sandwich box further with damp newspapers.

Meat

127   For the working person who wants to defrost meat for dinner: Take it out of the freezer in the morning and wrap it snugly in four or five sheets of newspaper. By late afternoon the meat will be thawed and still chilled, instead of mushy and warm.

128 One grated raw potato added to each pound of ground meat makes juicy hamburgers.

129 To cut meat into thin strips for stir-frying or Stroganoff, put the meat in the freezer for about 1-1/2 hours before slicing. It will cut easily into thin strips while it's partially frozen.

130 When broiling meats or bacon on a rack, place a piece or two of dry bread in the broiler pan to soak up the dripping fat. This not only helps to eliminate the smoking of the fat, but reduces the chances of the fat catching fire.

131 The higher the oven temperature, the more your meats will shrink. Simply by roasting them at no more than 300 degrees F to 325 degrees F, they will shrink less and be more tender.

132 Don't salt roast beef or steak until it is three-quarters cooked. It will retain its juices better if seasoned this way.

45

133 Cured meats can be frozen for only limited periods of time. A whole ham keeps for about two months; bacon, frankfurters, knockwurst, one month; corned beef, two weeks. Never freeze a canned ham in the can. Expansion during the freezing process could cause the can to burst.

134 To store meat in the refrigerator, remove the market wrapping. Recover it loosely with a large piece of plastic wrap. Do not wrap it tightly. The point here is to let the meat "breath." Store the meat on a plate in the coldest part of the refrigerator.

135 If you have leftover roast, but not enough to stretch it into another meal, slice the meat and make sandwiches. They freeze well for two or three weeks. But, please hold the mayo.

Bacon

136 To remove just the number of slices you want from a cold package of bacon, first roll the package up forward, then backward.

137 Bacon will be crisper if you pour off the fat continually while it's frying. It will lie flat in the pan if you prick it with a fork as it fries.

46

Money Savers

Coupons

138 There's nothing tacky about a collection of carefully clipped coupons presented at the checkout counter. Throw them away and you're throwing away money. Make them really count by trading coupons with friends. Those you reject can be another's treasures. If you don't use pet food, for instance, trade those coupons with a pet owner who can us them. Perhaps the pet owner will give you the coffee or cereal coupons they don't use.

Convenience Foods

139 It is **rare**, but some convenience foods actually do cost less than making them from scratch.

- Out-of-season vegetables and fruits are frequently cheaper frozen than fresh.
- Frozen French fried potatoes cost less than preparing fresh ones.
- Frozen orange juice costs about half the price of fresh.
- Some fish products are cheaper frozen than fresh.

In the Kitchen

140 Use a tea bag or two to make a pot of tea, adding your own sugar and lemon, rather than a ready mix.

141 Cube, slice or grate cheese yourself instead of buying it that way.

142 Buy large sizes of items when you can. Normally you'll save money. However, there are infuriating exceptions. You have to watch it. A pocket calculatior helps.

143 Buy day old bread and store it in your freezer. It keeps just fine for up to a month, and you may save as much as half on your bread bill.

Eggs
144 Some places actually sell eggs with brown shells cheaper than ones with white shells. They both have the same nutritional value and taste. Take advantage.

Cheese
145 If you are a cheese lover, spend your money on real cheese, not the blended, whipped, processed stuff with fillers added which is packaged in cute jars and exorbitantly priced.

If you crave a creamy, savory mixture, make your own. Let an 8 ounce package of cream cheese soften to room temperature. Stir it up a bit and thin it with a few spoonfuls of milk. Add herbs, shredded cheese, chopped bacon or onion to flavor it.

Chicken

146 If you are serious about fighting inflation in the kitchen, cut whole chickens up yourself, instead of buying them cut and paying a fat fee for a few minutes work. Here's a way to save even more. When fresh fryers are on sale, buy three. Disjoint and cut them into six boned breasts, six legs and six thighs. The breasts go into the freezer for a special dinner; the legs and thighs can be oven fried for dinner or lunches, or frozen for later. Everything else, plus scraps from boning, goes into a stock pot. Cover the scraps with water and add an onion, a stalk of celery, a bay leaf and a few peppercorns to the stock pot and simmer 2 hours. Strain it all into a colander and put the broth into the refrigerator. Tomorrow, remove all the fat that has hardened on top and boil down the broth, adding noodles, rice or vegetables for soul satisfying chicken soup. Take the meat off the remains in the colander and add it to the soup, make a casserole, sandwiches or even discard the whole mess. You are so far ahead of the game by now you can't lose. For a total cost of three chickens on sale, just consider the meals you've prepared at a sensational saving, with only a few minutes of work.

Kitchen Cleaning

Scouring Powder

147 You probably use twice the amount of scouring powder you need for a job simply because some containers have too many large holes. Cover half the openings with a piece of adhesive tape and see if the can doesn't last twice as long.

Bird Seed

148 If you feed birds in the winter, check out the price of the large 25 to 50 pound bags of seed. They usually cost one-third the price of the smaller 5 to 10 pound bags. Buy them at garden, building supply, or catalogue stores.

Tea and Coffee Stains on China

149 Tea and coffee stains can be removed from china with a soft wet cloth that has been dipped into baking soda.

Coffeemaker

150 Keep your coffeemaker scrupulously clean by rinsing it with water in which a few teaspoons of baking soda have been dissolved.

151 If you use a drip coffee machine daily, it requires a thorough cleaning at least once a month. Pour a solution made from equal parts of water and vinegar into the water reservoir and run it through the brew cycle. Then rinse your machine by running clean water through the cycle.

Thermos
152 Here's how to remove that musty smell from your thermos bottle: Fill it three-quarters full with warm water. Add 2 tablespoons of baking soda. Let the mixture stand in the thermos for 5 minutes or more. Swish it around a bit and then rinse the thermos out. Remember, never im-merse your thermos bottle entirely. It might cause the casing to come loose.

Blender
153 An easy way to clean your blender, instead of taking it completely apart, is to fill it one-quarter full with warm water. Add a drop of liquid dishwashing detergent. Cover the container and blend on a low speed for a few seconds. Then simply rinse it in cool water.

Wooden Salad Bowl

154   Your wooden salad bowl should not be washed but rubbed down with paper towels after each use and stored in the open air. If it becomes stained and sticky, sand it lightly with fine sandpaper, or wash it with denatured alcohol. Then wash it with a mild detergent and hot water. Rinse the salad bowl with water and dry it. Coat it with salad oil and store as directed above.

Cutting Board Care

155   A cutting board that is used for both raw meats and vegetables can become a breeding ground for salmonella, if not washed properly. Scrub your board well with a solution made from 1 tablespoon of chlorine bleach per quart of water. Rinse under very hot running water. Wipe dry with paper towels. Two boards, one for raw meats and one for vegetables, is a sensible idea.

Removing Fish Odors

156   Remove fish odors from dishes and utensils by adding a tablespoon of vinegar or ammonia to the washing water.

Sponges

157 Toss your kitchen sponges in the dishwasher when you do the dishes. It keeps them fresh and sanitized.

Nonstick Finishes

158 Here's a homemade solution for removing stains from nonstick finishes, such as Teflon: Boil a mixture of 1/2 cup of liquid bleach, 2 tablespoons of baking soda and 1 cup of water in the cooking utensil for about 10 minutes. Wash, rinse and dry the pan. Wipe it with vegetable oil before using it again.

Removing Price Stamps

159 To remove the purple-colored price marks that are stamped on many plastic goods, wipe the spot vigorously with plain rubbing alcohol. If these "lovely" marks get transferred onto your countertops, remove them the same way.

Sewing, Laundry & Clothes Care

Home sewers have come a long way from that painfully obvious "loving-hands-at-home" look, most of our efforts used to have. Modern sewing techniques, smart patterns from first-rate designers and a vast array of beautiful fabrics are all persuading the most chic women to sew for themselves. The quality of workmanship the home seamstress can achieve is, more often than not, better than is available at retail stores. The price tags placed on shabbily constructed garments are enough to send even drop-outs from the high school "Home Ec" class back to the sewing machine.

Most of us past adolescence have become convinced that a few really good clothes are more satisfying and even more economical, in the long run, than a lot of mediocre ones. And, when you plan on keeping clothes for more than a season or two, you had better pay some attention to the care you give them.

Perhaps you view fashion as superficial and frivolous. You may not have the slightest interest in sewing. However, for basic reasons, you should know the "ins" and "outs" of laundry and clothes care. After all, the way we look tells the world how we feel about ourselves.

Sewing

Scissors

160 Sharp-pointed scissors are a menace inside your sewing basket or drawer. Protect yourself and prevent damage to your container by sticking the point of the closed scissors into a cork.

161 Did you know "finger oil" will lubricate scissors? Rub each blade with your fingers frequently as you are using them. There's enough natural oil on you hands to give scissors the needed lubrication without risking oil drops on your material.

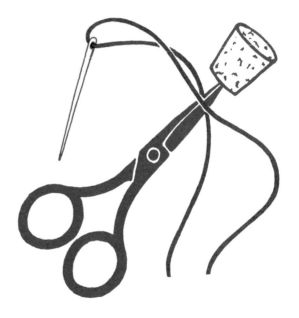

56

Pinking Shears

162   Perk up dull pinking shears by cutting several times through fine sandpaper.

Threading a Needle

163   When threading a needle, a dab of hair spray or spray starch applied to the end of the thread will stiffen the thread just enough to easily get it through the eye. If you don't have hair spray or spray starch, use clear nail polish.

Uncurling Thread

164   Thread that tends to curl and knot while you are hand sewing can be controlled. Rest a hot iron flat on the ironing board and draw a suitable length of thread under it. No more hassle.

Bulky Seams

165   Ever have trouble getting the machine needle to sew through heavy seams? Rub the seam with a piece of hard bar soap and you'll find it much easier.

Transfer Pattern Markings

166   To transfer pattern markings onto fabric, you can use a thin sliver of bar soap instead of commercial marking paper. It shows up clearly on almost all fabrics and, of course, comes off in the wash.

The Right Tape
for Pattern Adjustments

167   Pink hair setting tape is excellent for making adjustments on you pattern in place of masking or cellophane tape. Unlike other types of tape, it presses without a buckle or wrinkle when touched with a warm iron. It also works well to secure a pattern to leather or ultrasuede

while cutting them out, since these fabrics shouldn't be pinned.

Shopping for Buttons

168   This is one step better than merely taking a piece of the material with you when you shop for buttons. Cut three or four slits in the fabric sample so that you can slip the carded buttons through, making it easy to decide which size and color is best.

Sewing on Buttons

169   When you are sewing on buttons, double the thread before threading the needle. This makes four strands of thread used for each stitch taken. With this method, three stitches will attach a button quite securely.

Sewing on Snaps

170   To line up the two halves of a row of snaps, sew all the snaps with the points on one side first. Then rub chalk on them and press against the side where their mates must be sewn into place. The chalk will mark the places exactly.

59

Hemming a Skirt

171   Hemming a skirt is easier from the floor up. Mark a yardstick with a strip of bright tape at the ideal length from the floor. Hold your yardstick in front of you, end resting on the floor, and you can see at a glance how many inches to raise or lower the hem. After basting in the hem, it's wise to check against the yardstick again to make sure the hem is even.

Patches

172   When stitching on an important patch or insignia, apply it first with a dab of white glue. Let it dry and then sew around the edges by hand or machine. The glue will wash out.

Snags

173   That inexpensive, thin wire needle threader is a neat solution to the problem of snags in a polyester knit. Push the needle threader through from the wrong side of the fabric at the point of the snag. Catch the loose thread end in the tip of the threader; pull it back through the fabric and you have a smooth right side.

Magnet

174 A small magnet is a useful item in the sewing basket or drawer. Use it to pick up pins and needles that drop to the floor while you are sewing.

Pressing Velvet

175 Velvet must be pressed carefully. Put it right side down on a plush terry towel and press gently on the wrong side of the velvet.

Laundry

176 Before you wash any garment:
- Repair rips that may get worse in laundering.
- Shake out any loose dirt.
- Zip zippers, hook hooks and snap snaps.
- Remove belts and any trim you suspect will not wash well.
- Empty pockets.
- Pretreat heavy soil and remove stains.

Hand Laundry

177 When you've finished washing your hand laundry, let your washer complete the task. Place the clothes, still soapy and dripping wet, into your washer. Adjust the cycle to final rinse. Not only won't you have to rinse your fine washables, but you won't have to wring them either. Your clothes will dry much quicker too.

Chlorine Bleach

178 Chlorine bleach is well-known for its stain-removal ability. But did you know you should **never, never** mix it with ammonia or any other cleaning products? You could very easily create toxic fumes.

Soap vs. Detergent

179 Soap works fine for cleaning clothes in soft water but detergent is best for most water conditions. Hard water minerals combine with soap and form an insoluble scum that deposits on clothes and washer parts in an automatic washer.

Leave Yourself Notes

180   Ever wash a load of laundry and **THEN** remember an item you meant to put in with it, such as a robe, a blanket or a pair of tennis shoes? Leave a note to yourself right in the clothes hamper. Such efficiency is surely rewarded—somewhere.

Lint

181   If you're having a problem with lint on socks and other dark clothes, add a cup of vinegar to the final rinse cycle.

Socks

182   There are a lot of tips on how to keep socks together while you're washing and drying them. Pinning them together is one example. However, even after you've been diligent enough to pin them together, you're often still left with the irritating chore of turning them right side out. The solution to that is: return them to their owners "as is." Let **THEM** turn them right side out!

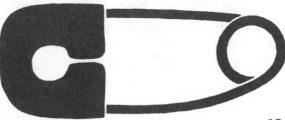

Silk

183   Dry cleaning is generally recommended for silk as the fabric tends to water spot. But some items, such as scarves, are hand washable. Use lukewarm water and a mild detergent. Rubbing is not necessary since silk releases soil very easily. After you rinse the item, wrap it in a bath towel to dry. Iron the item on the wrong side, while the garment is still slightly damp. Cover it with a white cloth to avoid water spotting and use the low setting of your steam iron.

Distributing Clean Clothes

184   Getting clean clothes back to their owners is accomplished easily with a shelf in the laundry area holding a rectangular plastic dishpan labeled for each member of the family. Even the little ones can take care of their own belongings this way.

JUSTIN

Removing Spots and Stains

185 Blood—For fresh stains, soak the garment in cold water first, and then wash in warm suds. If the stain remains, soak it in a bleach solution and rewash.

186 Candle Wax—Scrape off excess wax with dull knife. Put stained portion between paper towels; press with a hot iron. With stain face down on towels, sponge back with dry cleaning fluid. Launder.

187 Chewing Gum—Rub the gum with a piece of ice and scrape it off with a dull knife. Sponge with dry cleaning fluid and launder.

188 Chocolate—Soak the garment in cool water. Rub detergent on stain, then launder in water as hot as is safe for the fabric.

189 Coffee, Tea—Rinse in cold water at once. Then stretch the stained fabric across a sink and pour boiling water from a height of 2 or 3 feet through it. Launder and bleach the item if the stain remains.

190 Cosmetics—For lipstick, rub the stain with vaseline and wash in hot suds. Treat other stains with dry cleaning fluid; rub detergent on stain and launder.

191 Fruit and Wine—Soak in cool water. Stretch the stained fabric across a sink and pour boiling water from a height of 2 or 3 feet through the stain.

192 Grass—Rub detergent into stain; rinse and bleach any remaining stain. Launder.

193 Grease—Sponge with dry cleaning fluid; launder.

194 Ink—Rub the stain with white petroleum jelly or Crisco. Launder; bleach if stain remains.

195 Nail Polish—If fabric is not synthetic, sponge with nail polish remover or dry cleaning fluid; launder.

196 Paint—If stain has dried, soften first with vaseline; then sponge with turpentine until paint is removed. Rub in detergent, soak overnight in hot water and launder next day.

197 Perspiration—Sponge with detergent and warm water. Discolored fabric can sometimes be restored by applying white vinegar to old stains. Rinse with water. If stain remains, use dry-cleaning fluid, then launder.

66

Drip-Dry Rod

198   One of those adjustable tension rods made for closets or a round curtain rod makes a handy removable drip-dry rod for over the bathtub or in the shower.

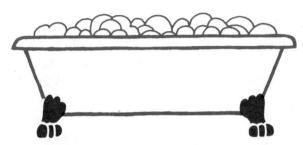

Quilts and Sleeping Bags

199   The bathtub is a good place to launder a sleeping bag or a quilt. Fill the tub about one-third full with lukewarm water; add a mild detergent. Place the item in the water and let it soak for thirty minutes. Squish the suds through it and rinse three times, squeezing **not twisting.** If you can let it drip over the tub for an hour on a line or a rod, you can keep squeezing out the water. After a good bit of the water has been removed, put it into the dryer on a low setting and toss in a clean pair of sneakers too. They will keep the quilt or sleeping bag from becoming overly fluffy.

Pillows and Dusty Draperies

200   You can give new life to pillows and dusty draperies. Put them into the clothes dryer (separately, of course) and toss them on the warm air cycle for about 15 minutes. It gets rid of lots of dust and delays expensive commercial cleaning. DON'T put foam pillows in the dryer.

Removing Starch from Iron

201   An easy way to get rid of starch on the soleplate of you iron is to iron over table salt sprinkled onto waxed paper.

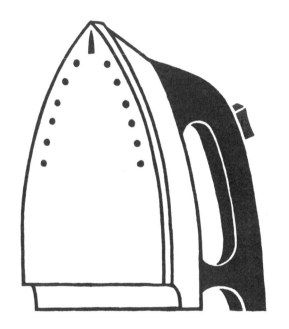

Clothing Care

Treating Clothes Properly.

202 Hanging your clothes on suitably shaped hangers, frequent use of a good clothes brush, and letting them air out before going back into the closet saves the need for routine dry-cleaning or washing. If you need an incentive, just consider the price of cleaning.

Knitted and Stretch Garments

203 Don't hang knitted or stretch garments to dry. They'll just keep on stretching. Most stretch clothes can be tumbled in a dryer. For those that cannot, squeeze them in a towel and lay them flat to dry. Even when dry, stretch garments shouldn't be hung for long periods. Store them flat in a drawer or on a shelf.

Clothes in Plastic Bags

204 You probably save the plastic bags from the cleaners to cover dresses. Here's an easy way to do that: Turn the bag upside down and put in the dress, on its hanger, with the opening at the top. Secure the bottom with a twist tie. Any dust on the floor of the closet won't fly in, and if the garment should slip off the hanger, it will fall in the bag, not on the floor.

Panty Hose

205   Panty hose will last longer when you put them on correctly. First sit down, then gather the entire garment together and slip each foot in so that toe and heel fit smoothly and aren't twisted. Then, with steady pressure and leaving no slack, draw hose up over the knees. Stand up and pull hose smoothly to the waist. If the panty part is still around your thighs, you are definitely buying the wrong size!

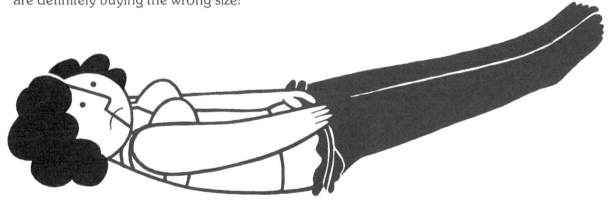

70

Alternate Your Clothing

206   Give the world a break, as well as your clothes. They will last longer if you give the wrinkles a chance to fall out, and the entire garment a chance to get back into its natural shape. Shoes, too, last longer when worn alternately with another pair. Perspiration is hard on leather; it needs a chance to dry.

When to Buy Shoes

207   Did you know that you should not buy shoes in the morning? By afternoon your feet can stretch as much as half a size.

Rain-soaked Shoes

208   Shoes that are rain-soaked should be stuffed solidly with paper and thoroughly rubbed with saddle soap while that are still wet. Let them dry with the soap on them and it will keep the leather from getting stiff. Be sure to wipe off the remaining saddle soap when they are dry.

Snappy Come-back

209   When your favorite fitting bra gets tired elastic or broken fasteners, you don't have to buy a new one. Instead, replace them with refreshers from the notions counter.

Health, Safety and Security

Remaining healthy, safe and secure is not easy today. Markets bombard you with products claiming to be "organic" and "natural." They sound good, and you may even feel obligated to buy them for your family. After all, they must be better than products that aren't similarly marked. Right? Wrong. There are no established or legal definitions for the words "organic," " natural," or "health food" when they appear on products of any kind. The fact is many packagers buy ordinary foods and label them as they choose.

Keeping your home safe and secure isn't easy either. We sometimes set ourselves up for an accident or a burglary as a direct result of our carelessness. Although these suggestions won't prevent all accidents or burglaries, they will make you aware of how to make yourself a lot less vulnerable.

73

Health

Health Foods

210 Be wary of food products labeled "organic," "natural" or "health food." There are no legal definitions and most of us are caught in the cross fire between the Food and Drug Administration, nutritionists and food faddists. The sad truth is, all kinds of packagers buy ordinary foods, label them "organic" and sell them at an amazing boost in price from the regular items. Your best protection is to:

1. Be suspicious of over-priced products.
2. Read the small print on labels.
3. Recognize an exaggerated claim when you see one.
4. Know the proprietor of the store you patronize.

Prescriptions

211 If you have trouble opening those new child proof bottle caps and have no children, you can ask the pharmacist to put your medicine in a screw-top bottle. Or, ask the doctor, when he's writing the prescription, to put that instruction on it.

Aspirin
212 Signs of spoiled aspirin are: a sharp vinegar-like odor when you remove the cap, fragments of loose powder, broken or chipped tablets. Even pure aspirin can lose its potency once the seal is broken.

213 When you open a bottle of aspirin, remove and discard the cotton wadding. If it's left in, it can collect moisture and that will accelerate spoilage.

Contraception
214 "No" is still the best oral contraceptive.

Vitamin C
215 Most of the vitamin C now being sold as "natural" consists almost entirely of abscorbic acid, exactly the same stuff you find in "unnatural" vitamin C. The difference is that the "natural" product frequently costs 50 percent more than the "regular" vitamin C.

Caffeine
216 If you drink five or more cups of coffee a day, you may be getting too much caffeine. Don't try total withdrawal. You may experience headaches, depression and fatigue. It's wiser to taper off gradually.

Diets

217 As an incentive for your diet, clip pictures of clothes you want to buy when you're slimmer and tape them to the refrigerator door. Also, tape a list on the door of treats you **CAN** have. No more standing there with the door open, mooning about what you can't eat and shifting things around.

Chapped Lips

218 Here's the best help for chapped lips. First place a warm washcloth over your lips for about five minutes to get water into the skin. Then apply a heavy coating of petroleum jelly. Repeat this several times during the day.

Burns

219 If you burn yourself while cooking plunging the burn into ice water is the quickest, safest way to relieve the pain.

Sunburn Treatment

220 Here's a sunburn treatment that makes you feel about as good as possible in that miserable circumstance: Take two aspirins and head for a tepid bath to which you've added a small box of baking soda.

Hypoallergenic

221 When you get right down to the nitty gritty, the word "hypoallergenic" doesn't mean much of anything on a cosmetic label. Once it was banned; now the word is back on labels, but it still doesn't mean the product is likely to cause fewer skin problems than another product.

Naps

222 Psychologists have determined that a short nap between noon and two probably won't affect your nighttime sleep, but a nap between 6:30 p.m. and 8:30 p.m. may leave you awake for the night. Consistent nappers will agree with Ogden Nash's sentiments:

> "Catnaps are too good for cats.
> I would not sell my daily swoon
> for all the rubies in Rangoon."

Reflective Tape

223   Make sure when children are outdoors early in the morning or after dark that they are easily visible. Reflective tape or patches sewn onto their clothing will allow drivers to see them more easily.

Adding Humidiy

224   One recommendation for fighting colds is to keep the humidity in your home at a comfortable level of 35 to 40 percent. A humidifier is the best way to do this, but you can also generate moisture in the house by boiling water on the kitchen stove or placing an open container of water near the radiators.

Shampoo

225   A shampoo once or twice a week with raw eggs will add bounce and life to the driest hair. Beat two eggs into 1/2 cup lukewarm water. Massage well into the hair and leave on for 15 to 30 minutes. Rinse out thoroughly with lukewarm (never hot) water. This is a protein-rich cleansing shampoo.

Cheap Tricks for Staying Warm

226 After a warm bath, don't pull the plug. Let the warm water and the steamy bathroom heat the rest of the house for a while.

227 When you finish using the oven and turn it off, let the door stay open. The hot air will warm the kitchen.

228 If you get cold enough this winter with your thermostat turned patriotically low, you won't snicker at this sensible reminder: A bare head can dissipate a large proportion of the body's heat. Wearing a hat around the house during the day and a nightcap in bed will make you feel much warmer. Sillier, perhaps, but definitely warmer.

Staying Cool
229   Some quick tricks for staying cool on hot days:
- Drink lots of water
- Eat lightly.
- Cover your head.
- Wear loose-fitting clothes in fabrics that breathe; cotton can't be beat.
- Powder your feet in the morning and once during the day.
- Run cool water over your wrists—your feet, too, if you can.

Sunglasses
230   When buying sunglasses, the experts say a neutral gray tint is best because it distorts colors least. They should be dark enough so that only 25% visible sunlight filters through.

Safety Appliances
231   Three basic steps to do IN ORDER when you have finished using an appliance:
1. Turn off the appliance.
2. Unplug it from the wall. Remember, a turned "off" appliance is still connected to electricity.
3. Disconnect the cord from the appliance, if that's possible.

Electrical shocks are possible if you don't follow these steps.

Precautions to Avoid Electric Shock

232 Never touch any electrical item—washer, dryer, drill, whatever—while you are barefoot or in wet shoes or sandals on concrete, stone, terrazzo, tile, metal or dirt.

233 Don't risk installing an antenna or mast if it could possibly fall near an electric service wire, if the day is windy or if you don't have enough help. Call for a professional under any of those circumstances.

234 Be especially careful in the bathroom handling any electrical device while you are wet.

T.V. Safety

235 A television set can be an electrical hazard. Some words to the wise:

- Always turn the T.V. off if you leave the room for more than a short period.
- Unplug the T.V. and disconnect the external lead-in wires when you leave on vacation.
- Be sure the ventilation openings aren't covered with cloth or papers, or are too close to a wall.
- Don't set any liquids on the cabinet. A spill could cause a short circuit.
- Never clean the face of the set while the T.V. is on. Any liquid that got inside could cause damage.

- If your cord shows signs of wear or damage, have it replaced.

Gasoline Storage

236 The first rule on storing gasoline is DON'T. But if you do, use an approved and labeled container. Keep it in a well-ventilated, closed shed away from the house and heat sources. Always fill a power mower or tank outside, never in your basement or garage.

82

Xmas Trees

237 If your Christmas tree is a cut, fresh one, try to stand it in a container of water. It will keep it from drying out so quickly, and reduce the chance of fire.

Electric Blankets

238 To get maximum efficiency from an electric blanket, you need a covering over the top of the blanket. Even something as thin as a sheet will hold in the warmth.

239 Even though electric blankets are electrically safe, it is not a good idea to use one on the bed of a child or invalid who might not be able to adjust the controls.

240 Launder, never dry clean an electric blanket. Cleaning solvent could ruin the insulation around the wires.

241 When storing an electric blanket, moth flakes or moth preventive spray could have a detrimental effect on the wiring. Better skip it.

Baby sitters

242 When you leave emergency phone numbers for the baby sitter, put your home address at the top of the list. In an emergency, sitters could forget the address of where they are.

Security

243 When you travel, leave a key with a good neighbor, for whom you can return the favor. Ask them to pick up your mail, go in to check things and watch the house. They are your most valuable security system.

244 Phone the police and tell them the dates of your absence. They are glad to check the house regularly.

245 Stop all deliveries ahead of time. Don't leave notes.

246 Any item of exceptional value should be put in a safety deposit box.

84

247 Arrange to have the grass cut.

248 Use timers and set them to have lights and radio go on to conform to your usual habits.

249 Have a neighbor park his car in your driveway frequently.

250 Don't tell everyone at the market, cleaners, beauty shop, garage, and local restaurant that you will be away. Talk when you come home.

251 Place a stick or broom handle in tracks of sliding doors and windows.

252 Adjust the telephone bell to its
lowest volume. An unanswered telephone
is a sure tip-off to an empty house.

253 A favorite security ploy used by some people is to remove complete drawers from their silver chest and move them to an attic or basement hiding spot or a safe. Then they leave a hand written note on the silver chest saying, "Dear John and Mary, Don't worry about the silver. Bill took it to our bank deposit box. Hope you enjoy using the house and can find everything. Love, Jean." Their theory is that a potential thief, seeing the note will decide there is no point in tearing up the house looking for silver, and that visitors could be arriving any time. Who knows—it doesn't hurt to try.

If you suspect theft
254   Never enter your house if anything appears even slightly suspicious. Go to a neighbor's home and call the police. A false alarm is better than interrupting a thief.

Etching Valuables
255   Police in many cities will lend you an etching tool that you can use to mark your valuables with your social security number. Prominently displayed decals noting your participation in this program might be discouraging news to potential thieves.

Locks
256   When you move into a different apartment or house, be sure to have all of the locks changed. Sounds unnecessarily expensive, but otherwise you will never know who else has a key to your home.

Women Living Alone
257   A woman living alone should make sure her telephone book listing and the name on her mailbox do not divulge the fact that she is living alone. List your name as J. Jones. Better still, list two names to make it appear you do not live alone.

The Home Executive

What is it about the word "executive" that the world seems to love? It is one of the most over-used words around, ranking close to "charisma" and "relationship." It is applied to housing developments, hotel rooms, clothes, toys, bathrooms and dining rooms. Its use as the title of these hints is much closer than those examples to the correct meaning: one with managerial ability; capable of carrying out plans and duties.

Much of the effort spent in running a home smoothly is done at the desk with a telephone and a checkbook. The one who pays the bills, makes appointments, keeps the records, and even plans for the dual inevitabilities of death and taxes deserves the title "executive." Some of the hints that follow will help you be a more canny consumer. All these skills add up to executive ability in my book. The reward for all this organizaiton? Merely peace of mind.

Get Organized

Files

258 There are so many records to keep organized in a home. A file box is the easiest way to accomplish this. It is handier than a bank deposit box and you will know exactly where to find tax files, insurance papers, health records, or other family documents you need.

Address File Cards

259 If your circle of friends is constantly on the move, you might prefer 3" x 5" file cards in a box instead of an address book. There is room to make changes, additions and subtractions.

Telephone Directory

260 Moving to a new town? Take along your current telephone directory. It will come in handy for contacting firms and friends after you've moved to give them your new address and to settle old accounts.

Inventory

261 An accurate inventory of your valuable possessions is a must. Taking photographs of antiques and other unusual items in the house is recommended as a means of receiving reimbursement from an insurance company following a loss.

Safe-Deposit Boxes

262   Legal experts advise against renting a safe-deposit box jointly. It's better to rent the box in the name of one person, usually the wife, with husband listed as a deputy. He would have full access to the box during the life of his wife. If he were to die, his wife would be able to open the box at her convenience, instead of the box being sealed pending a tax examination.

Your Will

263   A safe-deposit box is a good place for valuables, but **not** for your will. State law usually requires a safe-deposit box to be temporarily sealed in the event of your death. Your will should be at home, with your life insurance policies, or at your office. A copy should also be kept by your attorney.

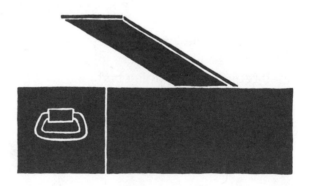

Mail

U.P.S. vs the U.S. Postal Service

264   When using United Parcel Service to mail a package to someone whose address is a box number, you might do a kindness by inquiring in advance whether it's more convenient for packages to be sent through the U.S. Postal Service or U.P.S. It can make a big difference. U.P.S. always gets a signature to prove delivery has been made. Since it cannot "deliver" to a box number, a postcard is mailed out and if a fuller address is not provided, the person getting the package may have to pick it up in person.

265   Since the United States Postal Service now requires the use of ZIP codes, they request that nothing be typed or written below the line showing the ZIP Code. The "Attention" line, formerly put on the lower left hand corner of the envelope, should now be typed two spaces above the name of the firm.

Mail Orders

266   When you are mail ordering an item and enclosing your check, put the firm's address on the check. You'll sometimes need that address handy when the canceled check comes back but the item you've ordered hasn't.

Special Delivery

267   Before paying for special delivery, ask at your local post office if it is available at the destination of the letter. In some remote areas letters go out with the regular delivery even though you've paid the extra fee.

Shopping

When to Buy

268 The least expensive time to buy:

Sheets and towels
  January and August "White Sales"
Lingerie
  January and August
Luggage
  July
Bathing suits
  July 5th
Furniture
  August

Christmas presents
  January
Cars
  August and September
Toiletries
  January and July
Costume Jewelry
  January

Catalog-Showroom Stores

269   You get no service, you fill out your own order form, you wait for the merchandise, and you carry it to the car yourself, but there's no question that a top value for many household purchases is at catalog-showroom stores. These are not like discount stores; there is only one of each kind of item on display and the merchandise consists of well-known brands only. When you know what you want and the brand you want, you should check out these showrooms.

Grocery Shopping

270   Put a time limit on your major weekly shopping trip to the supermarket and you are likely to save money. Surveys show if you shop for longer than 30 minutes you probably don't use a list and wind up buying unnecessary items.

271   Those mini-calculators are great for carrying around the supermarket. You can keep a running total on the grocery bill. And, in stores without unit pricing, it can quickly tell you whether the larger size is the economy buy.

95

Cash Discount

272 Under the Fair Credit Billing Act, some merchants who accept credit cards such as Visa and Master Charge are permitted (but not required) to give a discount to customers who pay cash. The law does not apply to merchants who issue their own credit cards. The saving is usually 5 percent, but it is up to you to ask whether the discount is available.

Prescriptions

273 Always ask your physician to give you the proprietary or generic name of a drug he is prescribing for you rather than a brand name. Then get on the phone and do some comparison shopping before you have the prescription filled. The drug will be identical, but chances are the prices quoted at several drugstores will not.

Advertisements

274 Through the maze of gadgets, gimmicks and "miracle" products you see advertised in the back of magazines keep two principles in mind:

- The offer of a money-back guarantee doesn't guarantee that the product is good.
- A product that sounds too good to be true is often worthless.

96

Poor Quality Products

275 What to do if a product doesn't live up to your expectations:

- Return it to the store where you bought it armed with the receipt and the item or its serial number. Be prepared to discuss exactly what is wrong with the product and whether you want it repaired, replaced or a refund.

- No luck? Next, call or write to the manufacturer's customer relations department. They usually have a toll-free number. Send photocopies (not originals) of receipts, canceled checks and other relevant information.

- Still no satisfaction? Write the president of the company. Look up his name at the library in **Standard and Poor's Register of Corporations.**

- As a last resort don't forget the "action line" type columns in your local newspapers. Especially when you have gone through all of the above steps and still have not received satisfaction, they will enter the fray and usually get some results.

Use Your Library

276   Your local library can be the source of all kinds of help when you are doing your best to fight inflation. All you have to do is ask. Here's a sample of what is there:

- Consumer advice.
- Ideas for better nutrition, low-cost meals and cooking techniques to save energy.
- Better gardens; techniques that can result in you cutting food costs.
- Investment advice.
- Records, tapes, sometimes even pictures for loan.

Consumer Reports

277   That classic shopper's guide "Consumer Reports" can be an invaluable tool for getting unbiased "best value" advice. It includes test results of products ranging from cars to contraceptives, for safety, convenience and effectiveness. Your local library has back files and also the yearly **Buyer's Guide** prepared by Consumers Union.

Toll Free Numbers

278   If a company you wish to contact has a toll free number, you can find it by dialing (800) 555-1212.

Handling Your Money

Savings Accounts

279 The ideal savings account is one that pays the maximum rate, compounds interest daily (or continuously) and credits interest daily to the day of withdrawal. Many institutions offer such accounts, but don't assume you will automatically get it.

280 Some people deliberately have too much taken out of their salary to avoid a large tax bill in April or to accumulate a refund. Those excess withholdings will do more for you in a savings account where they will earn interest.

281 Anytime you delay depositing checks, forget to cash traveler's checks after a trip or keep large amounts of cash around, you are depriving yourself of the opportunity to earn interest.

Prepaying Bills

282 Prepaying bills before they are due will not improve your credit standing. It only reduces the time your money can be earning interest.

99

Checks

283 Very cautious people keep their canceled checks separate from their unused checks. This keeps a thief from having at his fingertips both a sample of your signature and plenty of your checks with which to practice.

284 Never fill out checks for cash until you're ready to present them for payment. And never, never sign a blank check or give one to another person.

285 Whenever you write a check that is tax deductible, underline your signature with red ink and mark you check stub with red ink. When income-tax time comes, you'll be able to sort out your deductible items quickly.

Credit Records

286 Married women can have their own names listed on credit records, even when credit ratings are based on credit accounts held jointly with their husbands.

Credit Denial

287   If you are turned down for credit, you have a right to be told why. Ask the creditor which part of your report led to the rejection. You can then submit any additional information that shows you to be a better credit risk than they thought, or you can check your credit record yourself to see if there are any inaccuracies. If you ask the credit bureau to show you your file within 30 days after you are denied credit, they cannot charge a fee for disclosing your own record to you.

Credit Cards

288   Pay your monthly credit card bill in full if you possibly can and save those interest charges. When you pay only part of the bill, the credit card company is in effect lending you money—at an interest rate which is usually 18 percent yearly!

289 The easiest way to have a record of all your credit cards is to place the cards face down on a duplicating machine and make a few copies. If your wallet is stolen you have all the information you need. A good idea, also, while you're at the machine, is to copy any documents that are valuable and would be difficult to replace.

290 If you lose your credit cards, notify card issuers first. Some issuers have a 24-hour, toll-free telephone number for reporting lost cards. It's a good idea to have these numbers written on the record you keep of your credit card numbers. Once the issuer has received notice that a card is lost or stolen, you are no longer liable for unauthorized charges. Until then, you are responsible for charges up to a total of $50.00 per card.

Taxes

291 Relax! The I.R.S. isn't after you. Your profits from an occasional garage sale are not considered taxable income.

292 To be absolutely safe, save your tax returns and cancelled checks for six years. That is as far back as the I.R.S. will request information.

102

Your Home

Leaving in Style

293 Helpful information to leave the owner of the house you've just sold:

- Directions or booklets for the furnace and appliances you are leaving behind.
- Names of some close neighbors they can call when questions arise about the neighborhood.
- Any special treatment you give the house, plants and yard.
- The trash pick-up schedule for your street.
- Baby-sitters you know and recommend.
- A city map.

Scrapbook

294   Keeping a "house book" is a terrific idea. Notes on major home improvements, dates, costs and contractors name should be in it. Colors of wallpapers and paints, information on service for appliances and furnace; all will be helpful for insurance and tax purposes and a wonderful guide for a new owner should you sell the house.

Home Improvements

295   Home improvements you may love but that **WON'T** increase its resale value:

- Custom built facilities to store stereo equipment and odd size books.
- A special interest item like a sauna, greenhouse or darkroom—unless you just happen to find a buyer with the same interest.
- Exotic decor and landscaping. It may make your home appealing but is not likely to raise the resale value.

Renting
296 When you use an item only occasionally, it makes sense to rent it. Why buy and store a rollaway bed, a high chair, a punch set, a movie projector, tent, propane stove, electric hedge trimmer, carpet shampooer, adding machine—and so many more things—when you can rent them.

Saving Newspapers and Magazines
297 Old newspapers and magazines you want to save from mildew should be spread out to be thoroughly dry, sprinkled with cornstarch or talcum powder and placed in a manila envelope. Stow the envelope in a dry place.

Typewriter
298 Your "noiseless" typewriter will become even more so if you slip a foam-rubber backed placemat under the machine.

Masking Tape
299 Masking tape is handy for lots of things around the house: label packages stored in the freezer and mark with a felt-tip pen; keep track of when range hoods and furnace filters were last washed or changed with a strip of tape on or near them, marked with the date of service.

105

You Can Fix It

Billy Rose once said, "Never invest your money in anything that eats or needs repainting." If we were to follow that advice, we would all live alone in hotel rooms and order room service. Most of us, however, install ourselves and our families into some kind of house. It usually represents the largest single investment of our lives. While our families acquire regular and predictable eating habits, the house and everything in it seems to require upkeep and repair at inopportune times.

How can we survive this dilema? The answer is: learn to fix it yourself. You **can** care for and maintain you home in many instances. Such cleverness will hold repairmen at bay, reduce service calls and save one enough money to discharge that first responsibility—feeding the troops.

Appliances

Life Spans

300 If you know the number of years of service you can expect from an appliance, you can better decide whether it is worth fixing. Here are some approximate life spans:

Average Years of Service	
Clothes dryer	14
Clothes washer	11
Freezer	15
Hot water heater	10
Range	16
Refrigerator-freezer	16
Sewing machine	24
Toaster	15
Vacuum cleaner	15

Repair

301 Appliances on the blink are bad news. Keep those booklets that came with an appliance together in a file. They can give you good hints on repairing the problem yourself. If not, they usually bear the name of the store from which the item was purchased, often your quickest source of help. They also tell you the model number, or where to find it—something you'll need to report over the phone.

Self Cleaning Ovens

302 Chemical oven cleaner is **not** more economical than running a self-cleaning oven through its cycle. The porcelain used on the inside of these ovens can withstand high temperatures, but not strong chemicals. It only costs 15 or 20 cents to let your self-cleaning oven run through its cycle. It costs over 50 cents to use chemicals to clean your oven, plus a lot of elbow grease!

303 If you've ever thought of trying to clean your pots and pans in your self-cleaning oven while the cleaning cycle is on—don't! Most materials will melt, and if they don't melt there is the danger that accumulated grease in the pans will catch fire. Not a smart move.

Freezer Breakdown

304   If your freezer breaks down or turns off because of power failure:

- Keep the door closed. Opening it lets the cold air out and shortens your safety time.
- Food in a partially full freezer will stay frozen for a day; a full freezer holds for up to two days.
- If the freezer will be off longer, purchase some dry ice or transfer food to another freezer.

305   If the food has already thawed, use these rules to decide what to keep and what to discard:

- If food still has ice crystals in the center or is cold to touch, you can refreeze it.
- If meat, fish or poultry have warmed to room temperature, discard them.
- Warm vegetables and fruits that still smell good can be refrozen.

Furnace

306 The average life span of a well-maintained furnace is 20 years. Some give up sooner, but whatever the age of yours, you can reduce the possibility of trouble by having it checked out a few weeks before the cool weather begins. Don't allow strangers to give you a "free" inspeciton; there are plenty of con artists in this business. Call your utility company and ask for an inspection. Most of them do not charge for this service.

Air Conditioner

307 The secret of maintaining a trouble-free air conditioner is to check its filter every other week while it's in use. Your instruction manual will tell you where the filter is located. If your air conditioner is equipped with a permanent filter, wash it every other week. If it uses replaceable filters, replace them frequently. Keep several at home, so you don't have to run to the store each time you need one.

Overloaded Circuits

308 If the T.V. picture shrinks while you're ironing, if the mixer runs slowly, or if one fuse blows frequently, you have too many appliances plugged into the same circuit. A safe rule of thumb is to not have more than one heating appliance or two motor-driven appliances operating on the same circuit at the same time. Unplug the extra appliances, replace the fuse or reset the circuit breaker and start again, this time without an overload.

Potpourri

Hanging Pictures

309 You can decide where to hang pictures without marring the plaster if you have a "dry run." just cut out paper the size and shape of the pictures and pin them on the wall.

Tools
310 Rust can ruin your tools. If a spot appears, use a fine emery board or steel wool to remove it, then apply a thin coat of machine oil.

Toolbox
311 A piece of charcoal in the toolbox will absorb moisture and prevent rust.

Butcherblock Care

312 Butcherblock is such a popular material for kitchen counters and tables these days you should know how to care for it. If the wood is to be used strictly as a work surface and not for cutting, all you need to do is cover the wood with boiled (not raw) linseed oil. Let the oil penetrate for 10 minutes and wipe off with a soft, absorbent cloth. When scratches appear, sand them with a finely grained sandpaper, always working with the grain. Then re-oil the area.

Installing Draperies

313 If you are making curtains yourself, mount the drapery rods before taking the measurements. If you are buying the curtains, you do it just the opposite—install the rods according to the curtains sizes.

Wobbly Chairs

314 Do you have kitchen chairs that wobble? Remove the rung and scrape off the dried glue from the end of the rung and the hole. Apply a liberal amount of wood glue to both rung and hole and put the rung back in place. If the fit is still loose, thicken the glue with fine sawdust. It acts as a filler. Wipe away any excess glue before it dries

Drawers

315 If you have some drawers in your house that pull completely out when opened, attach two pieces of wood to the back of each drawer using small bolts and nuts. Twist the wood pieces to a horizantal position to install and remove the drawer; turn them vertically to stop the drawer as you pull it out.

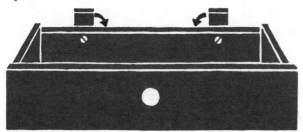

Batteries

316 Batteries from a camera flash unit, radio or flashlight that will not be used for long periods will last longer if they are kept cool. Seal them in plastic bags and place them in the refrigerator. The cool temperature reduces the continuous chemical reation in the battery cells.

Nailing Into Wood

317 You're less likely to split wood you are nailing into, if you first blunt the nail's point. Hold it upside down on a firm surface and tap the point with a hammer. Then, soap the nail before driving it through the wood.

115

Cleaning Golfballs

318   For the frugal golfer, here is a simple and easy method for cleaning old golf balls. Soak them overnight in a solution of 1 cup of water and 1/4 cup of household ammonia. Rinse them off with clear water and dry.

Firewood

319   You may see the "Ritual Fire Dance" performed right in your living room by an assortment of ants, cockroaches, spiders and termites if you don't take some precautions with your firewood. Old firewood that has been stacked a long time, can house a wide variety of pests that spring to life in a warm room. It's best to stack the wood away from the house on a bed of crushed stone or one of those iron hoops to keep it off the ground. Spray the wood with an insecticide, cover it with plastic and bring the logs into the house a few at a time, as needed.

116

320   You can pick up free firewood at most of our 154 national forests. The wood is from dead trees, logs lying on the ground and tops from logging operations. Call the Forest Service District Ranger's office. The number is listed under "U.S. Government, Department of Agriculture, Forest Service." That office will issue you a free use permit which specifies where to cut and any special rules and regulations. You must do the cutting and haul away the wood, but considering the price of wood, this is a good deal.

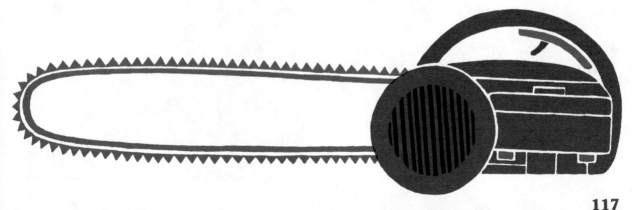

117

Power Failure

321 If you know ahead there will be a power cutoff, get yourself organized:

- Turn the controls of freezer compartments to "high" for maximum freezing.
- Fill your thermos bottles with soup or hot drink.
- Unplug large appliances and switch off all but a few lights once the black out starts. Lights going back on will tell you the blackout is over.
- By plugging your appliances in one at a time you reduce the danger of an overload and another blackout.

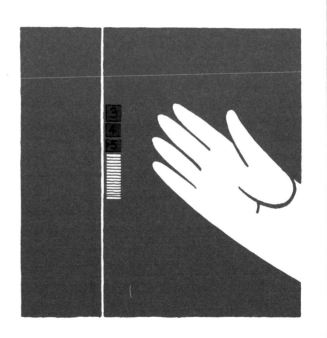

Painting

Brushes

322 A cheap paint brush just won't do the same quality work a good brush will. The difference is apparent in the finished job. And, poor quality brushes won't last as long as good quality ones.

323 When doing any painting or varnishing that is going to continue another day or week, you don't have to bother cleaning the brush each day. Just wrap it in foil or in a plastic bag and freeze it. When you're ready to resume painting, thaw the brush for half an hour before you need it.

Handy Paint Bucket

324 For a handy carry-around paint bucket, cut a good-sized hole in the top side of a plastic bleach bottle, opposite the handle. Be careful to leave at least four or more inches from the bottom of the bleach bottle up. That way there will be enough room for the paint. Leave the handle and the cap of the bottle intact. The bucket is light to carry and easy to get into with a paintbrush.

119

Magnets
325   A small magnet glued to the side of your paint can is a handy way to keep track of your wet paint brush. The magnet holds the brush securely as you move from place to place.

Use Light Colors
326   Think about using a light color when you plan on painting a room. It not only makes the room appear larger, but also has a positive, if small, effect on your electric bill. Light walls reflect more light back into the room, and a white ceiling gives you the maximum downward reflection from lamps!

Protect Light Fixtures
327   Use plastic sacks from the cleaners to wrap around your hanging light fixture to protect it from drips and splatters while you paint.

Painting Furniture
328   Nails driven part way into the bottom of the legs will hold a chair or table off the work surface, allowing you to paint the entire chair, including the bottom of the legs, at one time.

Scraping Paint

329 A single-edged razor blade is often used to scrape paint off windows, but your fingers soon become tired. Clamp the blade in the jaws of locking pliers. The handle gives you a good grip and a more comfortable angle from which to work.

Closing Lid

330 When the rim of the paint can is filled with paint and you're ready to tap down the lid, you can avoid the inevitable splatter if you place a cloth over the lid, then tap away.

121

Energy Savers

You won't save the world by throwing away your electric toothbrush but you can make a difference. There are energy eaters in a house that can be put on a diet if you will only think about it, change a few habits and take some precautions. Without any hardship, just thought, you can save energy, and that means dollars.

Someone once said the safest way to double your money is to fold it over once and put it in your pocket. If you take action on a combination of some of following ideas that apply to your home, you are guaranteed to be keeping more energy dollars in your pocket. These are basic, common sense hints, most of which won't cost you a cent.

Dishwasher

331 Skip the drying cycle and you'll save half the operating cost. Just open the door and let the dishes dry quickly. If you don't want the warm air in the kitchen, keep the door closed and your dishes will dry overnight. Some new dishwashers have a "no dry" cycle to save energy. If your's doesn't set a timer to remind you to turn off the machine before the dry cycle.

332 Run the dishwasher only when it is full. An average machine uses 16 gallons a load!

Stove

333 Use pans that are the same size as the burner to avoid wasting heat or adding extra cooking time. When possible, cook food covered to save energy and nutrients.

334 For electric surface cooking, turn the unit off a few minutes before the food is done. The stored heat will continue to cook the food.

Oven

335 For foods that require long cooking time, it is more economical to use the oven than the top of the stove.

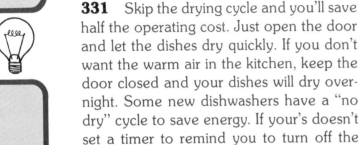

124

336 It is not necessary to preheat the oven for foods that will take more than an hour to bake.

337 When you're roasting meat, turn the oven off 15 minutes before the meat is done. The heat in the oven will finish the cooking—at no cost.

338 Unless it's necessary, don't open the oven to peek. You can lose 15 to 20 percent of oven heat each time you open the door.

339 Plan complete oven meals; many cookbooks are full of menu ideas. Remember, as long as the door stays closed, the oven is more efficient than burners on the range.

Electric Skillets

340 An electric skillet is a good alternative to an electric oven. It uses just half the energy and you can successfully bake potatoes, roasts and casseroles.

125

Washing Machine

341 Use a cold rinse in the washing machine. And, when possible, wash in cold water using a cold water detergent.

342 No more small loads. It is far cheaper to buy more underwear and socks than to wash more frequently.

343 A ten minute wash cycle is long enough to remove the soil from most clothes.

Refrigerator and Freezer

344 If you're buying a new refrigerator beware. The frost-free type uses twice the energy and costs about $45.00 more a year to run.

345 Don't allow a build-up to more than 1/4 inch of ice before defrosting it.

346 Check the seal on the refrigerator and/or freezer door by closing the door on a dollar bill. If the bill slides out easily, you need a new gasket.

347 Open and close the door of your refrigerator and freezer as quickly and as infrequently as possible.

348 Freezers and refrigerators both work best when full, but not tightly packed. The foods can keep each other cold.

T.V.
349 The "instant-on" feature is a huge energy user. If your set is this type, ask your hardware dealer for a "line-switch" suitable for a T.V. They are inexpensive and simple to install—and besides, will a minute's wait really inconvenience you?

350 A black and white set uses 60 percent less power than a color set.

Lights
351 Use fluorescent lights wherever possible. They give four times as much light for the money.

352 Use lower-wattage light bulbs wherever you can. Where you need more light, it is wiser to use a 100-watt bulb rather than two 60s.

127

353 Install a dimmer switch on ceiling fixtures. They let you lower the light level easily and can save up to half the electricity.

354 Dusting your electric bulbs may sound ridiculously fussy, but they burn 20 percent more efficiently if they are clean. Dust them automatically, every time you dust a room.

355 Turning off lights when you leave a room is definitely worth the trouble.

Water Use

Showers

356 Take showers instead of baths. It costs about half as much to heat the water for a shower as it does a bath ... **UNLESS** you stand in the shower longer than seven minutes. In that case, you'll save money by taking a bath.

357 Install a device that will reduce the flow of water through the shower head. It can cut water use in half without much noticeable change in water pressure.

Heating and Cooling Systems

358   Have both your heating and cooling systems checked every year to be sure they're working efficiently. It is best to have a trained serviceman for this job, but you can clean or replace filters every two months all by yourself.

359   Keep the thermostat at 68 degrees F when you are heating the house and 78 degrees F during the cooling season.

360   Keep vents closed to rooms you are not using and close the doors. Close closet doors. A lot of heat is wasted heating closets.

361   If you don't remove a window air conditioner during the winter, cover it tightly on the outside.

362   Open draperies during the day to let in free heat from the sun and close them on cloudy days and at night to keep heat from escaping. When you are cooling the house, close the draperies against the sun.

363   Tightening up the entire house with weatherstripping, insulation and caulking is of primary importance when you are spending money to heat it.

129

Gardening Indoors and Out

I know people whose houses could be rezoned from residential to "light jungle." They have meaningful relationships with their house plants and in the summer they can supply an entire neighborhood with zucchini and tomatoes.

Then there are those for whom a garden is a thing of beauty, but mostly a job forever. They buy flowers at the supermarket and dislike house plants because they think they suck up all the air in a room.

These hints are for the non-fanatic gardener, who wants to know a thing or two about potting a plant and how to make a bouquet last longer, but who likes mulching and misting in moderation.

It's clear that in the future, more of us will begin growing some of our own foods. Rising food costs, the yearning for fresh flavor, as well as the undeniable satisfaction of growing your own, are reasons for the ever increasing number of avid gardeners.

Indoors

More Water

364 Houseplants need **MORE** water if:

- The pot is clay.
- The light is bright and sunny and the temperature is above 65 degrees F.
- The stems are thin and woody and leaves are thin and large.
- The pot is filled with roots.
- The plant is mature.

132

Less Water

365 Houseplants tend to need **LESS** water if:

- The pot is plastic.
- The light is dim and temperature is below 65 degrees F.
- The stems are thick and have thick, succulent leaves.
- The plant has been recently transplanted.
- The plant is immature.

Hanging Plants

366 If your hanging plant has no saucer, put a plastic shower cap across the bottom of the basket while watering it. It looks silly but it will catch the extra water and save drips on the floor.

Drainage

367 If you want a lightweight drainage layer in the bottom of hanging planters, use the styrofoam leftover from meat trays and packing boxes instead of the usual gravel.

133

Plants in Plastic Pots

368   Plants in plastic pots need less fertilizer than those in clay pots. Green scum on the pots and white crust on top of the soil means the plants are receiving too much food.

New Plants

369   True house plant lovers say you should isolate a new plant from others for a couple of weeks to make sure it is insect and disease free.

Spray Bath

370   An easy way to give your house plants a refreshing spray bath is to put them all in the bathtub and spray away.

Increasing Humidity

371   Some plants, among them coleus, ficus, Christmas cactus and bromeliads, prefer a humidity of about 70 percent. In most homes in the winter months it is usually down to 25 to 40 percent. You can increase humidity by putting plants over the kitchen sink or in the bathroom. Grouping them together also helps because the air is usually more humid around several plants. Set them on top of a tray of gravel, sand or peat moss that is kept wet.

While You're on Vacation

372   Here's the best trick yet for keeping house plants alive and well while you're away. Water the plant well, then enclose it completely in a clear plastic bag from the cleaners or a clear painting drop cloth to cover a table of plants. Place in normal light and tie the bag securely top and bottom with string or a twist tie. You don't even have to take down your hanging baskets. Moisture collects and keeps the plant healthy for a month, we know for sure, and possibly longer. Warning: When you come home don't rip off the plastic bag abruptly or the plant will suffer shock. Untie the top and gradually let the plant adjust to the outside air for a day before removing the covering entirely.

373   Another way to care for house plants while you vacation, is to place the plants on bricks in a bathtub filled with 1/4 inch of water. Cover the tub with a large plastic sheet or drop cloth and seal the edges.

Repotting

374 When do you repot? Those roots will intertwine until they strangle themselves and kill the plant unless you know the danger signs:

- Roots poking through the drainage hole.
- Slight wilt after you water.
- Lower leaves are sickly yellow.
- Leaf size gets smaller.

Getting Potted

375 Take a piece of broken clay pot and put it over each drain exit in the pot you are using. (The English call this "crocking.") Place it with the curved outside "up" to allow water to drain under and out.

376 If you wish to set a pot with drainage holes in a decorative, glazed pot without a hole, add a one-inch layer of pebbles inside the larger pot to stand the smaller one on. Besides good drainage and being able to see if you plant is standing in water, it makes watering easy. You never have to worry about rings on the table.

136

377 If you plant directly into a pot without a drainage hole, begin with a layer of broken crocking pieces and pebbles. Then ad a half-inch layer of pea-sized charcoal and a pad of sphagnum moss or something similar. These layers should bring the level up to about one-third of the pot depth before adding the soil.

378 When you buy a plant, the greenhouse it came from may not have crocked it. If it hasn't been done, you should do so when you repot.

379 Whatever kind of container you are potting or crocking in, be sure it's clean. Use steel wool and warm water to wash out the remains of a previous plant. Dry the pot well before putting in a new plant.

137

380 Before You Get the Insecticide Try These Steps:

- Examine cut flowers and new plants brought into the house to be sure they are free of pests.
- Use sterilized soil for potting.
- Some insects may be washed from a plant with a lukewarm spray of water or a solution of 2 teaspoons mild detergent to a gallon of water.
- If only one or two plants are involved, you can handpick some insects off the plant or use a cotton swab dipped in alcohol.

"Homey" Treatments for Your Potted Plants:

381 Put several empty egg shells into a quart of water and let them stand for a day. Water your sick plants with this mixture.

382 To revive tired ferns, water them with 1/2 cup of salt added to six pints of lukewarm water.

383 Cold tea makes a good fertilizer for house plants and acts as an insecticide, as well.

384 If worms have infested your ferns, stick matches into the soil, sulphur end down. Four to six should do it, depending on the size of the pot.

Diagnosing the "Sickies"

385 General defoliation: Sudden change in temperature or light, transplanting shock or overwatering is usually the cause.

386 Browning of leaf tips: Probably due to overwatering or underwatering, but this also results from excessive fertilizing.

387 Spotted foliage: Overwatering is again the culprit in most instances, but also

check that the plant has not been burned from direct sunlight.

388 Leaves drop, shoots are dwarfed and branch repeatedly; also, new leaves are small: This usually means the plant has been injured by unburned cooking gas in the atmosphere.

389 No blossoms: Look for insufficient light, too high temperature at night, overwatering, poor drainage, lack of food or compacted soil.

139

390 Wilting: A general drooping can be caused by the pot standing in water or from not enough moisture. Perhaps the plant was in the sun or a warm place too long.

391 Hard, lifeless, sour-looking soil: Scrape away the top inch or two of soil and work around the roots with a small spoon. Apply a light top dressing of new soil or mix, the same depth as that removed.

Moderation

392   Keep your head in this whole house plant rage; you have your own life to live, too. If you look at house plants as attractive decorative accessories but aren't interested in more than routine tending, buy full-grown plants that are the right size for the spots you plan to put them. Water and fertilize them as necessary and when they become unattractive, replace them with new plants. Do not feel guilty.

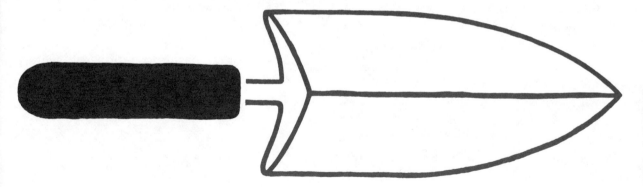

Keeping Flowers Fresh Longer

393 Neither a penny or aspirin dropped into a vase of cut flowers makes them last longer. Here's what will:

- Allow the flowers to stand in tepid water for half an hour.
- Cut one to two inches from the bottom of each stem at a slant.
- Remove all foliage that will be below the water line.
- Fill a clean vase with warm water mixed with a floral perservative available at florist and garden shops.
- Arrange the flowers and set the vase in a cool place for several hours of conditioning.

- Keep them in a cool place and not on top of the T.V. or near heat registers.
- Keep them away from fruits and vegetables, which give off a gas that flowers cannot tolerate.
- Check the water level daily and add fresh water as needed.
- Move them to a cool place or on the floor at night.
- Use a turkey baster to remove old water and add fresh without disturbing your flower arrangement.

142

From the Florist

395 A centerpiece from the florist is usually arranged in foam. Water is most often added before delivery, but not always. Check to make sure the foam is well soaked and if you need to add water, it must be warm, about 100 degrees F, because warm water is absorbed faster. Most florists supply a package of floral preservative with an arrangement that prolongs the life of cut flowers. Check the foam after several days and soak again if needed. If some flowers have faded, remove them, but most of the centerpiece should last many days.

396 When a box of cut flowers arrives from the florist they demand prompt attention. Recut the stems to open water-uptake cells. The cut can be straight across or on a slant.

Arrangements

397 Long-stemmed flowers in a wide-mouthed vase can be difficult to arrange. Make a criss-crossing of cellophone tape across the top of the vase to hold them in place.

Outdoors

Fertilizing With Kitchen Scraps

398   You can use kitchen scraps for plant food. Put them into a blender, add about three times again as much water and blend at high speed. Water the plants right from the blender before all the matter sinks to the bottom. You can use vegetable parings, lettuce leaves, eggshells, orange, lemon and grapefruit rinds—almost anything biodegradable.

Outdoor Cleanup

399   Make a quick cleanup for the outdoor gardener by tucking all those seemingly useless slivers of soap into an old nylon stocking or a mesh onion bag and tie it to the outdoor faucet.

Tools

400   During the months the garden tools are in frequent use, you may find it convenient to keep a bucket filled with sand mixed with lubricating oil so the tools can be dipped in for a quick cleaning and oiling.

Vines

401 When planting a vine beside the house you would be wise to buy or build an open-work trellis and set it about a foot from the wall. The trellis should be hinged at the ground level and fastened with bolts at the top. This allows you to detach the vine from the wall easily when the inevitability of painting or repairing the house arrives.

Forced Blooms

402 You can sometimes successfully force flowers into early bloom by pouring warm water around their roots.

Pest Attractors

403 Some plants, such as modern begonias, roses, strawberries, and cinerarias, are pest-attracting plants. If you are planning a low-maintenance garden you should be aware that they will make extra work for you.

Decorative Greens

404 Holiday time is pruning time. Fill your bowls, baskets and pitchers with evergreens clipped from your garden. Take the time to condition them and they will remain fresh many more days than they would otherwise. Cut off about one inch from each stem and remove foliage up about two inches. Place the stems in water with a few drops of liquid detergent and household bleach.

405 The Bare Basics of Pruning:

- Take off a stem or branch right above a growing bud that is pointed in the direction you want it to grow.
- If you want a plant to be bushier, take off the end bud.
- If a branch has only a few leaves, cut it off back to the main stem
- Stand back and look at the plant while you are pruning so you are sure to get the shape you want.
- Prune after flowering. In general this is late winter or early spring.

Vegetable Gardens

406 Most beginning vegetable gardeners plant too large a garden. You will do better with a small, well-kept plot than a large neglected one. The novice should start with a garden of about 10 x 15 feet.

407 This is a clever way to ripen vegetables in your garden faster. Use aluminum foil at the feet of your tomato, melon or squash plants, especially when the sunshine has been scarce. The foil reflects and gives off extra light which speeds ripening.

The Car

Tips for Economy, Convenience and Safety

In this world of uncaring gas station attendants and rising costs of automotive repair, it's smart to know how to do some simple maintenance yourself. If you know very little, or nothing about maintaining your car, you'll be surprised how uncomplicated the basics of maintenance are. By learning how to do a simple inspection of your car yourself, you'll not only save money, but perhaps even spot a potential problem before it happens. Although your inspections won't replace regularly scheduled, professional tune-ups, they can minimize the possibility of breakdowns.

Skyrocketing gasoline prices are affecting us all. Most of us now think twice before running errands or just going for a drive. We want to get every possible bit of mileage out of our car. There **are** ways to do it, too. You can make simple driving techniques become habits that will reward you with more miles per gallon than you thought possible.

Economy

Tune-up
408 A tune-up and oil change every 15,000 to 20,000 miles is the wisest money you can spend on your car for better fuel efficiency.

Tire Pressure
409 Too little tire pressure can reduce your gas mileage and tire life. Check the tire pressure once a month and always before a long trip.

Air Conditioner
410 Limit the use of your air conditioner to only the hottest days. It can reduce gas mileage by more than 10 percent.

Battery Water
411 Check the battery water once a week in hot weather and once a month in cold weather.

Wheel Balance
412 Have the wheel balance checked at tune-up time.

High Octane Gas
413 High octane gas has nothing to do with gas mileage. What it **can** affect is your car's operation. If the octane is too low for your car model the engine will not run as economically and could be damaged.

Steel Radial Tires
414 Steel radial tires can improve fuel economy by about three percent.

Maximum Efficiency
415 Most cars operate at maximum efficiency and economy between 30 and 35 mph.

Gas
416 Keeping your gas tank full at all times is wasteful. Each fill-up means there is the possibility of spillage and the additional gas weight also reduces gas mileage.

417 Manual transmission gives better gas economy than an automatic shift.

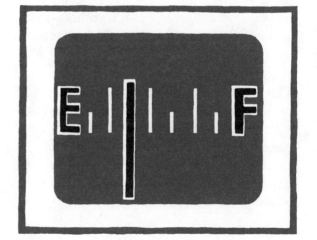

Consumer Reports

418 Next to knowing a superb mechanic who likes you and your car, the best economy advice a driver can get is in the monthly magazine "Consumer Reports." If you need tires, for instance, every garage or tire company you talk to will give you a different suggestion. "Consumer Reports" will tell you the best tire value for your particular car and your driving habits.

419 Jumpy starts and sudden stops use twice as much fuel as easy acceleration and smooth braking. To get into high gear quickly with an automatic transmission, lift your foot off the accelerator to make it shift earlier.

420 Use the brakes as seldom and as lightly as possible. Brakes waste the momentum your car has built up. Try to match your speed to the traffic speed.

421 Avoid idling your engine more than one minute when parked. It takes less gas to shut it off and restart it.

422 Maintain a steady speed. You get better mileage if you anticipate the green lights, hold your foot steady on the pedal as you ascend a hill and let off on the downgrade until speed is needed.

423 Combine the day's errands into one trip.

424 Observe the 55 mph speed limit on highways. It really does save gas.

425 Any car that requires unleaded gasoline, whether or not it has a catalytic converter, can use gasohol (90% gasoline and 10% ethyl alcohol) all the time. Other cars may require some lead to keep their valves lubricated, but you can usually substitute gasohol for leaded gasoline every **other** time you fill up.

For Your Convenience

426 Emergency Equipment

Even the most prudent driver has a limit to how much emergency equipment he can carry in his car. Here is a list of some of the best things to have on hand:

- White reflector tape. If a headlight burns out, paste some reflector tape over the lens as a safety measure.
- Baking soda. If a small fire starts in your engine or on your upholstery, sprinkle some baking soda over it. It should extinguish it quickly.
- Gloves. An old pair of socks or some gloves come in handy when a tire needs to be changed.
- Milk cartons. If you don't want to purchase flares, put two empty milk cartons in your car. They will burn for 15 minutes a piece.
- Thick rubber band. A thick rubber band will keep a flashlight securely attached to your wrist while you change a tire in the dark.
- Roll of paper towels. A roll of paper towels, kept in a plastic bag so they won't get damp, are useful to have. Use them to wipe up spills, hands, windshields and more.

For Those Who Wear Spike Heels:

427   Keep an old "right" shoe in the car under the driver's seat—something with a flat heel that you can slip into easily is best. A high heel can get stuck so easily under an accelerator. Plus, you'll avoid wearing a dirty smudge on the back of your good shoe.

Baking Soda in Ashtray

428   Endlessly helpful baking soda, once again is the source of a bright idea. Keep a layer in the ashtrays of your car to prevent cigarettes from smoldering and to reduce that stale smell.

A Reminder

429   A spring-type clothespin kept handy in the glove compartment can be clipped on the visor or the steering wheel as a reminder to turn off the headlights, or to get a quart of milk on your way home.

Dustmop

430   A dustmop head, worn like a mitten, is a great help for spreading suds and loosening grime when you're washing the car.

Garage Rash

431   If you have a narrow parking space, your car may suffer from garage rash: Chips and scars wherever the car door swings open and hits a wall. Tack up a strip of carpeting left over from your installation. You could use inexpensive carpet samples, also.

A Tight Fit

432   If your car has to fit into the garage just right, suspend a small rubber ball with string from the garage ceiling, hanging it so that it just touches the windshield when the car is pulled in far enough.

Safety

A Basic Checklist to Go Through Monthly

Tires and Wheels

433   Take a good look at the tire for blisters, pieces of tread missing, nails or glass in the tread, or scuffs and tears in the sidewall. Check tread wear. Tires should wear evenly. If they aren't, find out why; you might need new tires or a wheel alignment. A solid band of rubber showing where the tread should be means the tires are worn out. Look over the wheel rims for dried oil, which calls for a brake system check out, and dents, which mean whatever bent the tire may have affected your alignment. If you have any suspicions, ask your garageman to check.

Tire Pressure

434 Do this check when the tires are cool. Gas station gauges are not accurate so you ought to have one of those inexpensive, fountain-pen type tire gauges to do it yourself. The correct pressure is listed in your owner's manual or on the tire sidewall. Don't forget to check the spare tire.

Shock Absorbers

435 The car needs to be on a lift for a thorough check, but this will give you an idea. Push down firmly on each corner of the car, bouncing it up and down. If you stop bouncing but the car doesn't, the chances are good the shock absorbers are worn and need replacing.

Lights

436 Turn the ignition key to "ON" without starting the engine. Turn on your headlights, get out and walk around the car to check them on high and low beam. Then try the directional signals and the emergency flasher. You will need an assistant to check backup and brake lights. If any of them do not come on, the bulb or fuse has burned out. Your manual will explain where the bulbs and fuses are located and what kind you need if you want to replace them yourself.

Seatbelts

437   Look for any frayed spots that may have come from catching on a door. See that they fit properly and retract to take up the slack.

Steering Wheel

438   With the ignition switch on but the motor not running, hold the steering wheel with both hands and turn it left and right. There should be very little free "play" in the wheel.

Brakes

439   With the car in PARK and the parking brake on, step on the brake pedal. It should go down about half way and stop. If it continues to go down or feels spongy, have your brakes checked immediately.

Good Tires

440   Experts say the single easiest way to make your car safer is to put the best tires you can afford on it. Always use the recommended size tires for your car. Never use racing or agricultural tires on a passenger car.

30,000 Miles

441　A smart car owner automatically has belts and hoses changed at 30,000 miles. It won't add a dime to the total cost of maintaining the car because in the next few thousand miles they are going to start breaking on you. It makes sense to do it at your own convenience, not on the highway.

For Traction

442　Keep a bag of kitty litter in the car for wheel traction on ice. A few handfuls under the rear wheels can get you out of some slippery spots.

An Easy Under-the-Hood Checklist

The Maze
443 A look at all the wires and hoses under the hood can be formidable until you become familiar with it. Don't let it frighten you. The more often you look at it, the less complicated it becomes. Check for anything that looks loose, frayed or leaking.

Fluids and Oil Level
444 They should be checked every time you get gas. If you don't know how to do it yourself, how do you know they're doing it right? Here's how it should be done: Have something to wipe with. Pull out the dipstick, wipe it clean, re-insert it into the slot, pull it out again and read the oil level. It should read "full" or "near full."

Automatic Transmission Fluid
445 This is checked while the motor is running at an idle in PARK. Pull out the dipstick (you may have to ask the gas station attendant to tell you which one it is), wipe it, re-insert it, push it all the way in, and read it. If it is low you must replace the fluid, but don't overfill.

Radiator Coolant

446 This is checked on a cool engine. If you have a fairly new car you merely check the plastic jug next to the radiator to make sure the coolant is up the full level. On older cars you have to remove the radiator cap and this requires great caution.

Windsield Washers

447 The last fluid level to check is in the windshield washer reservoir. This tank should be kept filled. If the tank is filled and it doesn't squirt, the openings of the jets, located on your hood, may be clogged.

Belts

448 With the engine off, look at the belts that turn the fan, air conditioner and alternator to see they are tight and not frayed.

Hoses

449 Check to see there are no cracks, leaks or swollen spots. Replace **before** they cause trouble.

Some Danger Signals
that Could Lead to Trouble:

450 Cars usually give you plenty of warning before they give you big trouble. You will save money, in the long run, if you don't ignore a signal that something isn't quite right.

Warning Lights

451 If you continue to drive with a warning light flashing on your dashboard, you are asking for trouble. Go immediately to the first service station and locate the problem.

163

Noisy Muffler

452 The noise you'll hear when your muffler is malfunctioning is the least of your problems. The real danger is the exhaust gases which may leak into your car, and these are almost undetectable to your nose. If your muffler becomes noisy, have it checked at once.

Blown Fuses

453 Whenever your car blows a fuse, look for loose or exposed wires. Simply replacing the fuse may not mean you have corrected the problem.

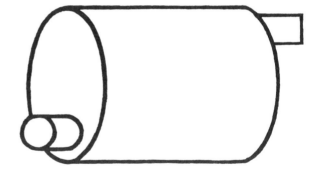

Bouncy Ride

454 If your car bounces a lot or nose-dives when you apply the brakes, chances are you need new shock absorbers.

Screeching Brakes

455   If your brakes squeal, they might just fail you when you need them most. Have them checked. Good brakes should operate with ease and feel the same each time you apply them.

Puddle Under Your Car

456   This could be a lubricant leaking from your car. Check the fluid levels on your oil, transmission fluid and coolant. In warm weather, condensation from the air conditioner will sometimes drip and form a puddle under your car. This is normal.

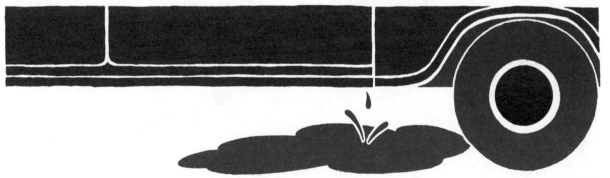

165

A Squeal Under the Hood

457   If this happens when you turn the steering wheel, the fluid in the power steering unit probably needs to be replenished. If you hear it sometimes when you are driving, it is probably a loose fan belt.

Growling From the Rear Wheels

458   Try coasting with the car in neutral. If the noise persists, it is probably the axle bearing. If the noise goes away, the trouble may be in the differential's bearing or possibly in the gears.

Knocking Under Acceleration

459 On older model cars this is a sign that the ignition timing is out of adjustment. This can lead to piston damage if you ignore the noise. On a newer car that uses unleaded gas, the knocking may mean that sooty deposits have collected in combustion chamber. A mechanic may be able to clean out some of the soot with a chemical cleaner, but you may have to switch to a higher-octane unleaded gas.

Travel

I've never understood people who can listen to the lyrics of "April in Paris" or Sinatra's suggestion to "Come Fly With Me" and not want to pack up immediately. For those of us who rarely travel, the **idea** of travel is romantic. The reality, I admit, can be far different. Glamorous lyrics and enticing ads never include swollen feet, lost luggage and the indignities of "being bumped."

Those who travel regularly, for business perhaps, know enough tricks and shortcuts that they are seldom caught by surprise. These tips will be old news to them.

It's the poor romantic who, despite his careful planning, can be disappointed and unprepared for the hazards of travel. These tips are for the romantic. They will save you from some common pitfalls and help you cope with the unexpected.

169

Luggage Tips

460 Identification tags are required on the outside of luggage on all airlines, but it takes something special to help you spot your luggage quickly when it comes by on the carousel. Mark it with bright colored tape or tie a yarn pom-pom or a sturdy ribbon on the handle.

461 Tape a business card or other identification on the inside cover of the luggage.

462 Don't overstuff a soft-sided bag so that it bulges at the sides. It could pop open in transit.

463 Call the airline in advance to find out where to get a carrier for a bike, skis, golf bag or other special objects.

464 Eliminate that tedious wait for your luggage at the end of a plane trip. For short jaunts (a week to ten days) you can get by with an under-the-seat bag and a garment bag. You carry on both bags; hang up the garment bag and stow the other under your seat. When you land you're on your way fast.

Fragile Objects

465   If you want to bring something fragile home in your suitcase, try packing it in an inflated plastic bag. Place the object inside the bag. Blow up the bag just as you would a balloon. Close it tightly with a twist tie or a rubber band. Cushion it between layers of clothing for added protection.

Zipper Bag

466   A zipper bag that folds flat is a handy item to have waiting in the bottom of your suitcase. You will usually need it for the trip home to carry dirty laundry, gifts, purchases, and the general overflow that seems to accumulate while one travels.

Plastic Bags

467   The plastic bag is your best packing aid: small ones for shoes, cosmetics and spillables; large ones for your most likely to wrinkle clothes. Pack garments in bags or place bags between clothes. They don't take up space and they keep a layer of air in to keep wrinkles out.

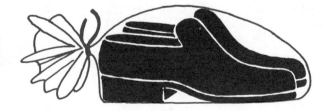

Flying

Comfortable Attire for a Long Flight

468   The most comfortable way for men or women to dress on a long flight is a jacket or cardigan worn over a skirt or pants, with a soft shirt or blouse, comfortable shoes and under it all, no tight-fitting underwear. With this you bring a "wonder" topcoat that may be reversable, is lightweight and does the job equally for day or evening wear. When you start your flight have the stewardess hang up your topcoat and jacket and put on a light weight sweater you have cleverly tucked into your carry-on-bag.

172

Avoid Prolonged Periods of Sitting

469   Prolonged sitting, as on a plane, can weaken muscles, stiffen joints and cause sluggish circulation at an astonishing rate. You can avoid the resulting headaches, backaches and swollen feet if you walk up and down the aisle as much as possible. Stretch frequently and do some tensing/relaxing exercises at your seat.

Sobering Thought

470   A warning on flying while flying: did you know at cruising altitude two drinks are equivalent to three on the ground?

Smoking Regulations

471   Smoking rules on airlines are clear. They are required to provide a no-smoking seat for every passenger who wants one, even if the entire plane has to be given over to accommodate nonsmokers. If you can't get a no-smoking seat, file a written complaint to the Civil Aeronautics Board. You may not get a refund, but the airline will be fined.

173

Getting Bumped

472 Getting bumped from a flight because it is over-booked has monetary compensations for the problems you are caused. You may be asked to volunteer for another flight and have the offer sweetened with cash. If you are bumped involuntarily, you will receive cash for your trouble, depending on the fare to your destination. If you take another flight that won't get you to your destination within two hours of the time you had originally planned, the airline should pay you double the price of your ticket. On international flights the time is four hours.

Film

473 Despite their claims, airport X-ray machines at the security checkpoint **can** damage film. One method of protecting your film is to have it hand inspected; it is your right to ask. To make this easier on you and the security inspector, you might carry your film, without box or can, inside a clear plastic bag. The other safe course is to buy a film shield bag that is lead-lined.

Overseas

Adjusting to Time Zones

474   The experts say it takes about 12 hours to fully adjust for each time zone crossed. It's smart to plan you schedule to allow for the adjustment. You can't fool your body's clock!

Travelers' Checks

475   Protect your travelers' checks by keeping a duplicate list of the numbers. Leave one list at home with a friend you can contact and carry the other with you— apart from your checks, of course.

Credit Cards

476   You can use your American credit cards abroad more than ever before. VISA seems to be the most widely accepted card, followed by Interbank (Master Charge), American Express and Diners Club. It is a good idea to carry more than one knd, just to be sure.

477   Since it can take months for those "plastic" purchases overseas to show up on your bill back home, it is almost like having a travel loan, interest free.

Foreign Currency

478 Protect yourself against dropping exchange rates by getting overseas vacation money changed to foreign currencies **before** you leave home. You can get forms to order foreign money and traveler's checks through U.S. travel agents.

479 Before you return home from an overseas trip, try to use up your local coins. You can exchange foreign bills for U.S. dollars at home, but usually not coins.

American Consul

480 When you travel abroad it's well to keep in mind what American Consuls

WON'T DO for you:
- Lend money or cash personal checks.
- Do the work of a travel agent.
- Arrange free medical service or legal advice.
- Provide bail or get you out of jail.

Overseas Calls

481 If you have to call the U.S. from abroad ask about surcharges before you call. Most hotels in Europe add a surcharge. It can double or triple the cost of the call. Use your telephone credit card, if you have one, or call collect. You may be able to minimize the surcharge.

Bibliography

Housekeeping

How to Clean Everything, by Alma C. Moore, $4.95. Simon and Schuster, New York.

The Formula Book, by Norman Stark, $5.95. Sheed and Ward, Inc., Kansas City.

Kitchen Smarts

The Supermarket Handbook, Access to Whole Foods, by Nikki and David Goldbeck, $7.95. Harper, New York.

Keeping Food Safe, by Hassell Bradley and Carol Sandberg, $7.95. Doubleday, New York.

Food and the Consumer, by Amihud Kramer, $6.50. Avi. Publishing Co., Conn.

Buying Guide For Fresh Fruits, Vegetables and Nuts, $2.00, by Blue Goose, Inc., Fullerton, California.

Laundry, Sewing and Clothes Care

The Stain Removal Book, by Max Alth, $6.95. Hawthorn Books, New York.

How to Recycle Old Clothes into New Fashions, by Fenya Crown, $8.95. Prentice Hall, New Jersey.

Singer Sewing Book, by Gladys Cunningham, $7.75. Golden Press, New York.

Health, Safety and Security

The Vitamin Book, by Rich Wentzler, $8.95. St. Martins Press, New York.

The Essential Guide to Perscription Drugs, by James W. Long, M.D., $8.95. Harper and Row, New York.

The A M A Book of Skin and Hair Care, edited by Linda Allen, $4.95. Lippincott, Philadelphia.

Security! How to Protect Yourself, Your Home, Your Office and Your Car, by Martin Clifford. Drake Publishers, New York.

Practical Ways to Prevent Burglary and Illegal Entry, by Val Moolman, $1.45. Cornerstone Library, New York.

Home Executive

How to Buy Everything Wisely and Well, by Bess Myerson, $9.95. Simon and Schuster, New York.

The Homeowner's Survival Kit; How to beat the high cost of owning and operating your home, $6.95. Hawthorn Books, New York.

The Dollar Squeeze and How to Beat It, by George Sullivan, $5.95. Macmillan, New York.

Supershopper; a guide to spending and saving, by David Klein, $5.95. Praeger, New York.

You Can Fix It

The Family Handyman Home Improvement Book, by the editors of The Family Handyman Magazine, $14.95. Scribner's, New York.

The Homeowner's Minimum Maintenance Manual, $6.95. Evans & Co., New York.

McCall's How to Cope With Household Disasters, by the editors of McCalls, $7.95. Random House, New York.

Complete Book of Home Repairs and Maintenance, by Jackson Hand, $8.95. Popular Science Publishing Co., New York.

Energy

Tips for Energy Savers, from U.S. Dept. of Energy, Editorial Services, 8G-031, Office of Public Affairs, Washington, DC 20585, free.

Weatherproofing, by the Editors of Time-Life Books, $7.95

Heating Your Home With Wood, by Neil Soderstrom, $3.95. Popular Science, New York.

Garden

Making Things Grow Outdoors, by Thalassa Cruso, $7.95. Knopf, New York.

How to Grow House Plants, by the Sunset Editors, $2.95. Lane Publishing Co., California.

Gardening For Food and Fun, Supt. of Documents, Washington, DC 20402. #0001-000-03679-3. $6.50

More Food From Your Garden, by J. R. Mittleider, $7.95. Woodbridge Press, Santa Barbara.

The Car

The Whole Truth About Economy Driving, $5.95. HP Books, Box 5367, Tucson, Arizona 85703.

The Time-Life Book of the Family Car, by the editors of Time-Life Books, $14.95. New York.

The Backyard Mechanic, Vol. I, 001G, $1.25 and **The Backyard Mechanic, Vol. II,** 002G, $1.60. Consumer Information Center, Pueblo, Colorado 81009.

Travel

Facts and Advice for Airline Passengers, Aviation Consumer Action Project, Box 19029, Washington, DC 20036. $1.00.

The Total Traveler by Ship, by Ethel Blum, $7.95. Travel Publications, Inc., Miami, Florida.

Mobil Travel Guides, to all areas of the United States, revised annually, $4.95. Rand McNally, Chicago.

Fieldings Travel Guide to Europe, $10.95. Fielding Publications, New York.

Index